Separate but Equal:
The Desegregation of America's Schools

Lucent Library of Black History

Anne Wallace Sharp

LUCENT BOOKS

An imprint of Thomson Gale, a part of The Thomson Corporation

THOMSON

GALE

379.263
SHA

Detroit • New York • San Francisco • New Haven, Conn. • Waterville, Maine • London

© 2007 Thomson Gale, a part of The Thomson Corporation.

Thomson and Star Logo are trademarks and Gale and Lucent Books are registered trademarks used herein under license.

For more information, contact
Lucent Books
27500 Drake Rd.
Farmington Hills, MI 48331-3535
Or you can visit our Internet site at http://www.gale.com

LIBRARY OF CONGRESS CATALOGING-IN-PUBLICATION DATA

Sharp, Anne Wallace.
    Separate but equal : the desegregation of America's schools / by Anne Wallace Sharp.
        p. cm.—(Lucent library of black history)
Includes bibliographical references and index.
ISBN-13 978-1-59018-953-5 (hard cover : alk. paper)
ISBN-10 1-59018-953-1 (hard cover : alk. paper)
1. School integration—United States—History—Juvenile literature. I. Title. II. Series.
LC214.2.S52 2006
0379.2'63--dc22

2006008269

Printed in the United States of America

Contents

Foreword   4

Introduction
Centuries of Discrimination   6

Chapter One
Jim Crow: Separate but Unequal   10

Chapter Two
A Landmark Decision   21

Chapter Three
The South's Fight Against Desegregation   37

Chapter Four
The North: De Facto Segregation   52

Chapter Five
Breaking the Color Barrier on College Campuses   65

Chapter Six
The Resegregation of America's Schools   81

Notes   93
For More Information   98
Index   100
Picture Credits   104
About the Author   104

Foreword

It has been more than five hundred years since Africans were first brought to the New World in shackles, and over 140 years since slavery was formally abolished in the United States. Over 50 years have passed since the fallacy of "separate but equal" was obliterated in the American courts, and some forty years since the watershed Civil Rights Act of 1965 guaranteed the rights and liberties of all Americans, especially those of color. Over time, these changes have become celebrated landmarks in American history. In the twenty-first century, African American men and women are politicians, judges, diplomats, professors, deans, doctors, artists, athletes, business owners, and home owners. For many, the scars of the past have melted away in the opportunities that have been found in contemporary society. Observers such as Peter N. Kirsanow, who sits on the U.S. Commission of Civil Rights, point to these accomplishments and conclude, "The growing black middle class may be viewed as proof that most of the civil rights battles have been won."

In spite of these legal victories, however, prejudice and inequality have persisted in American society. In 2003, African Americans comprised just 12 percent of the nation's population, yet accounted for 44 percent of its prison inmates and 24 percent of its poor. Racially motivated hate crimes continue to appear on the pages of major newspapers in many American cities. Furthermore, many African Americans still experience either overt or muted racism in their daily lives. A 1996 study undertaken by Professor Nancy Krieger of the Harvard School of Public Health, for example, found that 80 percent of the African American participants reported having experienced racial discrimination in one or more settings, including at work or school, applying for housing and medical care, from the police or in the courts, and on the street or in a public setting.

It is for these reasons that many believe the struggle for racial equality and justice is far from over. These episodes of discrimination threaten to shatter the illusion that America has completely overcome its racist past, causing many black Americans to become increasingly frustrated and confused. Scholar and writer Ellis Cose has described this splintered state in the following way: "I have done everything I was supposed to do. I have stayed out of trouble with the law, gone to the right schools, and worked myself nearly to death. What more do they want? Why in God's name won't they accept me as a full human being?" For Cose and others, the struggle for equality and justice has yet to be fully achieved.

In many subtle yet important ways the traumatic experiences of slavery and segregation continue to inform the way race is discussed and experienced in the twenty-first century. Indeed, it is possible that America will always grapple with the fallout from its distressing past. Ulric Haynes, dean of the Hofstra University School of Business has said, "Perhaps race will always matter, given the historical circumstances under which we came to this country." But studying this past and understanding how it contributes to present-day dialogues about race and history in America is a critical component of contemporary education. To this end, the Lucent Library of Black History offers a thorough look at the experiences that have shaped the black community and the American people as a whole. Annotated bibliographies provide readers with ideas for further research, while fully documented primary and secondary source quotations enhance the text. Each book in the series explores a different episode of black history; together they provide students with a wealth of information as well as launching points for further study and discussion.

Introduction

Centuries of Discrimination

From the earliest decades in the history of the United States, Americans recognized the importance of education. Learning to read and write was seen as necessary if men (and later women) were to participate fully in society. Black Americans were just as aware of the importance of education, yet more often than not they were denied access to even the most basic schooling. "The Black community," opine historians Joseph L. White and James H. Cones III, "recognizes education as a powerful tool that can equip people to meet the challenges of life effectively. However, educational institutions in America have uniformly failed them."[1]

For African Americans the primary obstacle to obtaining an education was racial segregation. White Americans used segregation and discrimination to maintain their supremacy over black Americans in all phases of life, including education. Even after the federal government committed itself to protecting their rights, African Americans were routinely discriminated against in employment, public services, and education.

Early Discrimination in Education

From colonial times, educational opportunities for African Americans were extremely limited. In the southern states in the decades following the American Revolution, slave codes made it illegal to teach slaves to read and write. White southerners felt they had good reasons for such restrictions. Historian Leon P. Litwack elaborates, "Slaveholders, legislatures, and courts deemed black illiteracy essential to the internal security of the white South."[2] These codes and laws were strictly enforced, often with violence. In spite of this obstacle, as many as 10 percent of slaves did learn to read and write, although most often they had to teach themselves those skills.

Blacks fared little better in the North, where whites often saw to it that schools were strictly segregated. Some African Americans attended separate black schools that were financed by white abolitionists or religious groups like the Quakers. In many areas,

White educator Prudence Crandall (shown) defied convention when she admitted a black student to her boarding school in 1832.

This woodcut shows a grade school for freedmen in 1866 in Vicksburg, Mississippi. Many blacks were denied education for decades after the Civil War.

what education was available to blacks was offered in schools opened by other blacks. Many whites simply believed that there was no reason to educate blacks.

Attempts to Desegregate

Not all whites believed education should be kept from blacks. One of the earliest attempts to desegregate a school came in 1832 in Canterbury, Connecticut, when a young white educator named Prudence Crandall admitted an African American to her previously all-white girls' boarding school. The parents of the white students immediately protested and withdrew their children. Not to be deterred, Crandall opened the Young Ladies and Little Misses of Color School, with twenty students. The townspeople of Canterbury reacted with outrage to this attempt to create a school for blacks in their neighborhood. Shopkeepers refused to sell goods to Crandall; other whites would throw eggs and stones at her and the students. In response to the demands of Canterbury residents, the Connecticut legislature passed a new law that forbade out-of-state blacks from attending Connecticut schools. Crandall was ultimately arrested for disobeying the law. Although she won her case on appeal, while she was in jail, the townspeople had burned the schoolhouse to the ground. Crandall had no money to rebuild and was forced to abandon her effort to educate blacks.

Another challenge to segregation came in 1849, when Benjamin F. Roberts, a black man who was active in Massachusetts's Anti-Slavery Society, tried on four different occasions to enroll his five-year-old daughter in an all-white school in Boston. The school board repeatedly turned down the application, so Roberts sued the school board. His attorney argued that "the separation of the schools, so far from being for the benefit of both races, is an injury to both. It tends to create a feeling of degradation in the blacks, and of prejudice and uncharitableness in the white."[3] Unfortunately for Roberts, the argument failed to persuade the court, which held "that there is no principle of state law guaranteeing African Americans treatment from government equal to that accorded whites."[4]

As a result of these and other prohibitions, by the mid-nineteenth century the number of educated blacks in the United States was low. On the eve of the Civil War in 1860, for instance, out of a population of five hundred thousand African Americans in the United States, fewer than thirty thousand attended school and these were, for the most part, living in the North. The Civil War would result in the end of slavery, but it would be nearly a hundred years before the nation seriously addressed the question of whether schools should be available to everyone, regardless of race.

Chapter One

Jim Crow: Separate but Unequal

The end to slavery in America, along with constitutional amendments that guaranteed all Americans equal protection under the law and the right to vote, created unprecedented opportunities for blacks. African Americans knew that education would help them make the most of those opportunities. Yet few schools were open to both blacks and whites, and those that were open to blacks were, by design, inferior to those open to whites.

Following the Union victory in the Civil War, during Reconstruction, the newly freed slaves flocked to schools throughout the South and elsewhere. Hundreds of black adults and children registered for schools that had been opened by the federal agency known as the Freedman's Bureau. While also providing some assistance to white southerners left destitute by the war, the bureau's main emphasis was on helping African Americans obtain an education and find jobs. Less than a month after Union troops occupied Richmond, Virginia, in 1865, for instance, more than one thousand African American children and nearly one hundred adults were attending newly opened schools.

By 1870 nearly three thousand schools were providing education to more than 150,000 African American students in the

South. Most of the teachers in these schools were northern white women, many of whom belonged to the American Missionary Society. Their aim was to serve what they saw as both the educational and spiritual needs of their students. The job these women did was not an easy one as they faced prejudice from local whites who wanted the former slaves to remain subservient. Intimidation and violence from southern whites were a constant reality for these teachers.

Plessy v. Ferguson

The end of Reconstruction in the mid-1870s heralded the end of any federal efforts to provide or enforce equal opportunities for blacks, especially in the South. White supremacists wasted no time in ensuring that blacks would return to a status that, while technically free, amounted to little more than bondage. By the end of the nineteenth century many of the gains African Americans had made during Reconstruction, including those in education, had been reversed. Hundreds of schools for blacks were closed, leaving only about one-third of all African American children in school. In addition, blacks were being prevented from voting and holding public office, were denied many basic public services, and were relegated to the least desirable sections of trains and other forms of public transportation.

The hopes of African Americans for the same opportunities whites enjoyed came to an abrupt end in 1896. That year the U.S. Supreme Court decided a lawsuit brought by Homer Plessy, an African American from Louisiana who had been jailed and fined for refusing to sit in a train car reserved for blacks. At issue was the Fourteenth Amendment, which had guaranteed all citizens equal protection under the law. Justice Henry Billings Brown wrote and delivered the majority opinion:

> The object of the [Fourteenth] amendment was undoubtedly to enforce the absolute equality of the two races before the law, but in the nature of things it could not have been intended to abolish distinctions based upon color, or to enforce social, as distinguished from political equality, or a commingling of the two races upon terms unsatisfactory to either.[5]

Jim Crow

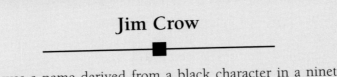

Jim Crow was a name derived from a black character in a nineteenth-century minstrel show. This derogatory term was eventually applied to the laws and customs that were created to keep African Americans subjugated. In the early twentieth century the southern states wrote numerous Jim Crow laws into their constitutions that mandated segregated or separate facilities, as well as segregated education, employment, and housing for blacks.

Blacks in the South were reminded on a daily basis of their second-class citizenship by signs such as "No Colored Allowed" and "Whites Only." While segregation was most visible in the South, African Americans who lived in the North were also victims of discrimination. Until the latter half of the twentieth century, blacks were blocked from most hotels, restaurants, and public facilities throughout the United States.

The Jim Crow era was also characterized by intimidation, threats, and violence against African Americans. Blacks were the victims of thousands of lynchings and murders. Black schools, homes, and entire communities were burned out. Despite protestations from blacks and whites alike, the court system and the federal government did little to punish the offenders or address the wrongs being committed.

Originally a stereotypical caricature of a black minstrel, Jim Crow came to signify enforced racial segregation.

By ruling against Plessy, the Supreme Court opened the door for the legal principle of "separate but equal," which would guide American race relations for the next sixty years. As long as facilities for blacks were equal to those reserved for whites, the Court had said, segregation was legal. White southerners hastened to write this principle into their laws and state constitutions, in essence forbidding blacks to mingle with whites in schools and elsewhere. The *Plessy* decision ushered in the Jim

Crow era, a time that saw discrimination against African Americans reach new heights.

White Supremacy

Underlying the segregation and discrimination of the Jim Crow system was the belief that whites were superior in every way to African Americans and all other races. Any mixing of races threatened that superiority. White southerners, in particular, believed that the separation of blacks and whites was essential to their own survival as the dominant race.

The beliefs of white southerners were supported by several popular theories of race that emerged at the beginning of the twentieth century. Many renowned scientists had espoused the theory that blacks and other "people of color" were inherently inferior to whites. These theories held that nonwhites were incapable of

The southern states segregated blacks from whites in all aspects of life including public facilities such as separate drinking fountains.

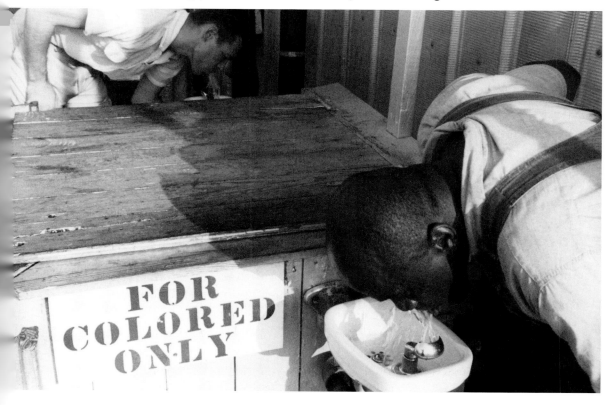

advancing beyond a basic kind of existence; they were, thus, unworthy of being treated equally to whites, let alone being allowed to mingle freely with them.

White southerners believed this was especially true in the field of education. As part of the *Plessy* decision, the Supreme Court justices had said that it was perfectly legal to establish separate school systems for the two races. The Court had stated, "The establishment of separate schools for white and colored children . . . has been held to be a valid exercise of . . . legislative power."[6] Southern legislators took advantage of the decision to create a dual system of schools.

Part of the motivation behind these laws was the fear on the part of white southerners that an educated black person might want a more equal role in society. "They acquire uppishness, they begin to swell, and to fancy that they are equal to whites," stated one white politician in the South. "If you educate the Negroes, they won't stay where they belong"[7] Many whites also believed that with education, black people would be less willing to work for whites. With the southern economy dependent in large part on black labor, this was clearly unacceptable. As a result of these concerns, southern legislators worked feverishly to create barriers to education for African Americans.

Benjamin E. Mays, a black minister and the president of all-black Morehead College, elaborated about the impact of the Jim Crow laws: "The first objective of segregation [and the Jim Crow system] is to place a legal badge of inferiority upon the segregated. . . . The second objective . . . is to set the segregated apart so that he can be treated as an inferior. . . . The third objective . . . is designed to make the segregated believe he is inferior."[8] Segregated education, in large part, accomplished all of these objectives.

The Inequality of Black Education

One way segregation reinforced the idea that blacks were inferior was that the separate schools for black children were inferior to white schools, even though the Supreme Court had ruled in *Plessy v. Ferguson* that facilities must be equal in every respect. "No matter how it was measured—by the quality of the facilities, the length of the school term, financial appropriations, student-teacher ratio, curriculum, teachers' preparation and salaries," historian Litwack explains, "the education available to black children in the . . . South was vastly inferior to that available to white children."[9]

Limiting public funding of black education was one of the primary ways that white southerners inhibited the education of African American children. Black schools were allocated little public money. Nearly 70 to 80 percent of all funding, in fact, was used for white schools. This left little to provide even the basics for black students. Whereas most white schools, for instance, had buses, black children often walked long distances to school. White students got new textbooks, but black students used out-of-date, tattered books. Many schools for whites were being built during the Jim Crow era, but schools for blacks were not. Existing buildings were simply allowed to deteriorate.

Little effort was made by white school boards to find qualified teachers for African American schools. As a result, in the majority of black schools the teachers had little more education than their students. Ray Sprigle, who visited the South during the Jim Crow era, writes of his experience there: "Hundreds of southern Negro schools have teachers who never went beyond the sixth or seventh grade and are wholly unfitted for teaching."[10] In many parts of the South, moreover, qualified white teachers were forbidden by law to teach black children.

Making matters worse, salaries for black teachers were extremely low compared to those for white teachers. In 1945, for instance, the average black teacher in Mississippi was paid $33 a month, compared to $150 for white teachers. It has been estimated that nearly one-fourth of African American teachers left their jobs each year because of low pay. Black parents often had to supplement teacher salaries and pay for materials that white children routinely received through public funding.

What the schools taught black students was aimed at furthering white supremacy. White public school officials in the South designed the curricula for all schools—black and white. The textbooks were written to emphasize the supposed inferiority of blacks. African Americans were frequently characterized as an ignorant and helpless people who were unable to survive without the help of a benevolent—and superior—white society. As a result of these stereotypes, black children, already living in a segregated society that placed them in an inferior position, learned little that challenged their status in society. Historian David R. Goldfield explains, "The black child came out of the public school system handicapped for life in the 20th century, but generally suited to assume his position [an inferior one] in the American South."[11]

Many African Americans sought to challenge the inequalities in education throughout the early twentieth century. In Mississippi, for instance, black teachers formed the Mississippi Association of Teachers in Colored Schools as early as 1906. Twenty years later, African American parents in that state created the Mississippi Congress of Colored Parents and Teachers. These groups repeatedly petitioned the Mississippi legislature for funds to improve black schools; those funds were just as repeatedly denied. "Throughout the South," Litwack concludes, "the story of black schools became a case study in deliberate and criminal neglect."[12]

Jim Crow Schools

That neglect included the buildings themselves, where African American children were often forced to endure deplorable conditions. Sprigle, in his article "A Visit to a Jim Crow School," describes such a school:

> This dilapidated, sagging old shack, leaning and lop-sided as its makeshift foundations give way, is the lordly white's conception of a schoolhouse for Negroes. . . . The warped old clapboards are falling off. Holes bigger than your hand give permanent cross-ventilation. There are no desks . . . a few dog-eared school books are scattered on the tables. A blackboard, apparently home-made, just a sheet of cardboard about two by three feet, is nailed to the bare studding.[13]

Most schools had no desks or chairs. Instead, students sat on benches of raw, unfinished pine with no backs or simply bales of straw. The books were often worn out and covered with doodles and racial epithets. One student recalled that black youngsters spent the first week of school erasing the most offensive language. Many schools lacked running water and bathrooms; children often had to go into the woods to relieve themselves.

Highlander Folk School

■

Established by Myles Horton in Grundy County, Tennessee, in 1932, the Highlander Folk School was initially a training school for labor organizers. As time passed, however, the founders of the school changed their focus to concentrate on the discrimination and racism that were evident throughout the country, especially in the South. By the late 1940s the school had narrowed its emphasis and decided to specifically address the issue of segregation in public schools.

Highlander provided a gathering place for those interested in social change and civil rights. In 1953 the school initiated a series of programs and summer workshops with the goal of helping black and white representatives of civil, labor, church, and interracial groups to lead the move toward school desegregation. At least half the workshop attendees were black. These groups gathered to work on strategies for achieving the desegregation of schools in their individual communities. Many of the Highlander students later became powerful figures in the civil rights movement.

In April 1960 police officers raided the school in Monteagle, Tennessee, and accused teacher Septima Clark of illegally selling beer. In the court case that followed, despite the fact that the state presented no evidence to support the charges, the court closed the school and confiscated its land.

A 1940s photo of Martin Luther King Jr. at the Highlander Folk School was used years later in this billboard.

The NAACP Targets Education

Such conditions attracted the attention of the National Association for the Advancement of Colored People (NAACP), which had been created in the early twentieth century for the purpose of addressing the inequality that existed between blacks and whites. According to its constitution, the NAACP was founded "to achieve, through peaceful and lawful means, equal citizenship rights for all American citizens by eliminating segregation and discrimination in housing, employment, voting, schools, the courts, transportation, and recreation."[14] From early in its history, the NAACP recognized that the best way to attack segregation might be to focus on the inequalities that existed between the teaching of black children and whites. The NAACP hoped that once discrimination was ended in the schools it would be easier to end it elsewhere.

To carry out its strategy, the NAACP established the Legal Redress Committee, later renamed the Legal Defense and Educational Fund. Charles Hamilton Houston, a brilliant lawyer and dean of the Howard University Law School in Washington, D.C., was chosen as the chief counsel of this committee. Houston immediately adopted two criteria for accepting cases to be argued in court. First, the case had to involve discrimination and injustice; second, it had to be broad enough to establish a legal precedent, thus serving as an example for similar cases in the future.

Together with his most promising student, Thurgood Marshall, Houston decided that the NAACP's first attack would be on the segregation that was practiced in the graduate and professional programs at many universities. Houston knew that black college graduates had little opportunity to advance beyond the level of a bachelor's degree because the majority of white graduate schools refused to accept African American applicants. "The two men concentrated first on graduate and professional schools," historians explain, "believing that white judges were most likely to be offended by segregation in that setting and to sympathize with the ambitious young black college graduates who were plantiffs in the cases."[15]

Important Milestones

Houston and Marshall mounted the first major challenges to segregation at the university level in the 1930s and 1940s. One of

Thurgood Marshall (standing) prepares a desegregation case with Charles Hamilton Houston (far right) in 1935 against the University of Maryland.

the first cases, *Sweatt v. Painter*, challenged the constitutionality of the University of Texas's refusal to admit an African American to its law school. Rather than allowing Sweatt to attend the University of Texas, the state had created a separate law school just for him. Now the *Plessy* decision, which had approved the idea of separate-but-equal schools, worked to Thurgood Marshall's advantage. He argued that this separate school, with its one student, two teachers, and no library, was in no way equal to the law school reserved for whites. On June 5, 1950, the Supreme Court agreed with Marshall and ordered Sweatt admitted to the University of Texas.

A second case, *McLaurin v. Oklahoma State Regents*, served to ensure that black students really had equal access to previously segregated schools. The case was heard by a federal district court in 1948. George McLaurin had applied to the University of

Oklahoma's graduate school of education and was denied admission. The district judge ordered the University of Oklahoma to admit McLaurin. Historian Goldfield explains what happened next:

> The university administration, determined to enforce segregation in some form and perhaps hoping to discourage McLaurin and other blacks from challenging the system again, forced McLaurin to sit at a desk in an anteroom outside his classroom, provided a segregated desk in a dingy corner of the library, and allowed him to use the cafeteria only at odd hours and to eat only at a specific table.[16]

McLaurin's case ultimately went to the Supreme Court, where the justices ruled that the university's restrictions were unconstitutional. Chief Justice Fred Vinson wrote that "the restrictions placed upon him [McLaurin] were such that he had been handicapped in his pursuit of effective graduate instruction. . . . State-imposed restrictions which produce such inequalities cannot be sustained."[17]

While these two cases did not challenge segregation at the elementary or high school levels, they were, nonetheless, important milestones in the fight against educational discrimination. These decisions called into question the idea that separate facilities could ever be equal and set the stage for the cases that would follow.

Chapter Two

A Landmark Decision

After the successes of the graduate college cases, the NAACP and its legal team, now headed by Thurgood Marshall, decided the time was right to challenge public school segregation directly. Public opinion about discrimination against African Americans had undergone a subtle shift during World War II and the years that followed. A groundbreaking book, *An American Dilemma: The Negro Problem in Modern Democracy*, by Swedish economist Gunnar Myrdal, had presented a horrifying picture of the Jim Crow system. Though condemned in the South, the book had been widely read in the North, causing many of its readers to question the morality of segregation.

Adding to the growing public concern about discrimination in the United States was the fact that American troops—including black soldiers—had just fought a war with Germany, supposedly to restore freedom to the people of Europe. The fight for democracy and equality in Europe and elsewhere made it more difficult for Americans to argue that segregation and discrimination at home were acceptable. In addition, segregation tarnished the reputation of the United States at a time when the nation was vying with the Soviet Union for influence among the newly independent nations in Africa. The United States could

Swedish economist Gunnar Myrdal, who exposed the horrors of Jim Crow segregation in a best-selling book, speaks on U.S. economic policy in 1979.

no longer ignore the plight of American blacks and expect to have its model of democratic government taken seriously elsewhere.

As they considered the state of their own democracy, Americans had only to look at the statistics to realize that school segregation was a significant problem in many parts of the United States. In the early 1950s, for instance, there were more than 2 million African American children attending segregated schools throughout the South and elsewhere. Historians Stephen and Abigail Thernstrom elaborate, "Black and white children were required to attend separate schools by state law in all the Southern and border states, and by an edict of Congress in the District of Columbia."[18] Many of these laws were written into state constitutions, such as this one in South Carolina: "Separate schools shall be provided for children of white and colored races, and no child of either race shall ever be permitted to attend a school provided for children of the other race."[19]

The shift in attitudes about segregation did not, however, extend to America's schools. A Gallup poll, taken in the 1940s, had indicated that 98 percent of all whites in the South, and 40 percent of those in the North, favored segregated schools. Because of this, the NAACP's attorneys knew they faced a difficult challenge. Still, they began a concerted search for cases that were clear-cut enough to be appealed to the U.S. Supreme Court.

"We Negroes Have Caught Hell Long Enough"

One of the first cases that came to the attention of Marshall involved Clarendon County, South Carolina, where the population was nearly 70 percent black. The county had more than sixty

In 1979 Harry Briggs stands in front of the Clarendon County, South Carolina, school he challenged in an unsuccessful desegregation lawsuit in 1949.

small black schools, most of them dilapidated shacks and barns, and no school buses. During the 1949–1950 school year, Clarendon County spent nearly two hundred dollars a year for each white student, compared to only forty-three dollars per year for each black one. Clarendon's black parents decided to sue the county over this inequity. At the very least, the parents hoped to force the county to provide a bus to transport their children to school.

When Thurgood Marshall learned of this situation, he approached the parents and told them that the NAACP wanted equal treatment in all aspects of public education, not just bus transportation. He asked them to find twenty black families willing to sue the Clarendon County School Board. At this point, the NAACP still was not prepared to directly challenge segregation itself; the suit Marshall wanted the families to file only asked for equal, not integrated, schools.

The plaintiffs were led by a black minister and schoolteacher, Joseph Albert DeLaine, along with Harry Briggs, whose children attended one of the schools. As a result of being involved in the lawsuit, both men faced reprisals. DeLaine was fired from his teaching job, and his wife, two sisters, and a niece lost their jobs as well. Someone set fire to his church, and the county's white firefighters stood and watched as it burned to the ground. Briggs and his wife also lost their jobs. Historian Sanford Wexler explains that these were the well-known consequences for challenging southern segregation: "For blacks to join in a lawsuit against the school board meant risking their jobs and losing their bank loans and their farms."[20]

Despite the repercussions, the group persevered. Rebecca Brown, a black grocery store owner, spoke for many South Carolina African Americans when she stated, "The Court has got to cut this segregation out, because we Negroes have caught hell long enough."[21]

Thurgood Marshall represented the plaintiffs before a South Carolina court. He argued that the black schools were inferior in every way to the white ones and concluded with these remarks: "The Negro child is made to go to an inferior school; he is branded in his own mind inferior. This sets up a road block to his mind which prevents his ever feeling equal."[22] Despite Marshall's arguments, the South Carolina court ruled in favor of the county school board. The situation for the African American children in Clarendon County did not improve—no new black schools were built, buses were not provided, and the inequality in access to educational resources continued.

The NAACP lawyers did not let this defeat or deter them, knowing that any long-lasting change would have to come at the national, not the state or local, level. Marshall and his team kept the case on hand as part of their effort to gather a number of cases that could eventually be appealed to the Supreme Court.

A School Walkout

Shortly after the Clarendon County case was decided, word reached Marshall that a group of African American students had taken action against discrimination in Prince Edward County, Virginia, at the all-black Robert R. Moton High School. As was often true of black schools, Moton was overcrowded, and the school board made no move to ease conditions. Instead of allowing some of the African American students there to attend a near-by white school, the county school board scheduled classes in Moton High's auditorium, in an old bus on the school grounds, and in three flimsy and hastily constructed buildings. Moton also did not have a gymnasium or cafeteria and was prohibited by the school board from offering several subjects commonly found in white schools, such as geography, world history, algebra, and geometry.

In April 1951 sixteen-year-old Barbara Rose Johns and nine other black students took matters into their own hands by escorting their teachers out of Moton High and calling a strike. Soon other students joined in, staying out of school for three days to protest the overcrowding and inadequate facilities at their school. When the conditions at Moton High School, along with the actions of these students, came to the attention of the local NAACP branch, it sent lawyers to talk with the students and their parents. All agreed that the NAACP should sue Prince Edward County, not for a better black school, but for the right of black students to attend school with their white counterparts.

In Virginia district court, NAACP lawyers Spottswood Robinson and Oliver Hill tried a new tactic to bolster their case. For decades, white southerners had used what they claimed was black inferiority as a rationale for not providing better schools. Robinson and Hill hoped to show that any such inferiority was the product of segregated schools and had nothing to do with race. To do so, the attorneys called M. Brewster Smith to testify on their behalf. Smith, a young social scientist and chair of the psychology department at Vassar College, testified that there was a growing body of evidence that school environment rather than racial heritage was the primary factor affecting a student's learning ability. The defense responded with its own expert, Professor Henry Garrett, chair of Columbia University's Department of Psychology, who testified that his experience had shown that blacks were inherently inferior.

The court ruled for the commonwealth of Virginia, and no changes were made at Moton High School. Once again the NAACP legal team set the case aside for future action. Furthermore, the lawyers felt somewhat satisfied that they had challenged the concept that African Americans were inherently inferior and thus incapable of learning. Realistically, however, Marshall and the NAACP knew that they were not yet ready to challenge the separate-but-equal laws. More cases were needed to buttress their claim that separate could never be equal.

A Small Victory

Two cases in the state of Delaware allowed the NAACP to move closer to its goal. The first was *Belton v. Gephart*, the other was *Bulah v. Gephart*. In both cases, the plaintiffs were asking that their children be allowed to attend nearby white schools rather than being forced to attend inferior and less-convenient black schools.

Both cases were argued by NAACP lawyers Jack Greenberg and Louis Redding. Chancellor Collins Seitz of the Delaware Supreme Court ruled that, despite the black schools being clearly inferior, he could not overturn the concept of "separate but equal" that had been set forth in the *Plessy* decision. Seitz did, however, order the white schools to admit black students. This was the first time a segregated white elementary school and high school were ordered to admit black students. This small victory gave further impetus to the NAACP in its determination to challenge school segregation.

Protesting overcrowded conditions, students gather in the auditorium of Robert R. Moton High School in Prince Edward County, Virginia, in 1951.

Linda Brown and the Kansas Case

The best known of the cases that would eventually come before the Supreme Court was the one involving seven-year-old Linda Brown of Topeka, Kansas. Despite the fact that there was a white school only seven blocks from her house, Linda had to walk miles through a train yard and across a busy intersection just to reach her bus stop. Her parents, Oliver and Leola Brown, like other African Americans in the neighborhood, feared daily for their daughter's safety. Their concern eventually persuaded them to contact the local chapter of the NAACP for help.

The NAACP responded to the Browns' request by gathering thirteen concerned black parents from the Topeka area and asking them to take their children to the closest school on the first

Linda Brown (front row, right), the child at the center of the historic *Brown v. Board of Education* decision, sits in her Topeka classroom in 1953.

day of classes, even though those schools were reserved for whites. When all the black children were denied admission to the all-white elementary schools, the NAACP filed a lawsuit. The Kansas courts eventually upheld the school board's actions, ruling that the white schools did not have to admit black children.

Still, the ruling gave the plaintiffs some hope. While the court did not overturn the legality of segregated schools, the Kansas judge did, nonetheless, make a remark that Thurgood Marshall would later use to present his case before the Supreme Court: "Segregation of colored children in public schools has a detrimental effect upon the colored children—the impact is greater when it has the sanction of the law—for the policy of separating the races is generally interpreted as denoting the inferiority of the Negro group."[23] This was the very point that Marshall and the NAACP had been trying to make in court from the beginning.

"It Stigmatized an Entire Race"

By the fall of 1952 the NAACP legal team decided it had what it needed to move ahead with appeals. The lawyers gathered these four cases and prepared to petition the U.S. Supreme Court to hear them. The cases were accepted by the Court and were eventually grouped together under one name: *Brown v. Board of Education of Topeka, Kansas.*

Marshall and his staff spent months preparing for their appearance before the Court. They wrote long legal statements, called briefs, along with oral arguments in which they would present the legal points they were trying to make. The team also gathered witnesses who would testify about the negative effects of school segregation on African American children. Eventually, a 235-page brief was submitted to the Court, signed by hundreds of noted lawyers and historians throughout the United States, all supporting an end to segregated education.

What all the cases had in common was that African American children had been denied admission to white schools and forced to attend schools that were clearly inferior to those reserved for whites. In directly attacking the separate-but-equal theory, Marshall was challenging the theory that separate facilities, including schools, were appropriate. Marshall's task therefore, was to prove that separate facilities could never be equal and, furthermore, that to subject African Americans to inferior conditions was damaging to them as humans.

Marshall knew, however, that proving school segregation was harmful to African American children would not persuade the Court to overturn the *Plessy* decision, so he planned to base his case on the Fourteenth Amendment, which states that all American citizens are entitled to the equal protection of the law. Historian Robert Weisbrot elaborates on Marshall's strategy: "Marshall argued that segregation was inherently unconstitutional for it stigmatized an entire race and thereby denied it equal protection of the laws as guaranteed by the Fourteenth Amendment."[24] Segregation, he argued, resulted in the black students being shortchanged in every way.

To prove that segregation actually hurt African American children, Marshall and the other attorneys utilized the findings of a number of sociologists and psychologists. The research conducted by psychologist Kenneth Clark played a pivotal role. Clark and his wife, Mamie Phipps, had tested black children in Washington, D.C., and in New York City. Using dolls—two black and two white—Clark asked the African American children which doll was better. Unanimously, they chose the white ones. When asked to pick the inferior doll, the children uniformly chose the black ones. What the tests revealed, Clark said, was that a sense of racial inferiority began early in life and was reinforced during the child's years in school. He stated, "These children saw themselves as inferior, and they accepted the inferiority as part of reality. . . . These children . . . have been definitely harmed in the development of their personalities."[25]

The Supreme Court Deliberates

The Supreme Court justices who heard the *Brown* case were deeply divided on the issue of segregation and the constitutionality of the "separate but equal" idea. After hearing the initial arguments from the opposing attorneys, they were unable to arrive at a majority decision. On June 8, 1953, nearly a year later, the case was held over, meaning that the Court would hear new arguments during the next term, which would begin in October 1953.

At this point events beyond anyone's control intervened. Shortly before the Court reconvened, Chief Justice Fred Vinson, a strong proponent of segregation, died. Earl Warren, the former governor of California, was chosen by President Dwight D. Eisenhower to take his place. The Court heard the additional arguments in December. The justices then retired to their chambers to consider the matter. Over the next few months Chief Justice Warren, who favored desegregation, was very clear with his colleagues on how he wanted the decision to come out: He wanted a unanimous decision ending school segregation. Warren reasoned that such a ruling would help keep desegregation from becoming a divisive force on the Court and the nation. Warren met individually with each justice. Knowing he already had the support of several justices for his position, he concentrated on those who supported segregation. Using a variety of methods, including a little arm-twisting along with an appeal to their religious and moral values, Warren convinced his colleagues to vote unanimously for the end of school segregation.

Thurgood Marshall

Born in Baltimore, Maryland, in 1908, Thurgood Marshall experienced segregation as a youth and would later devote his life to ending discrimination. He attended all-black Lincoln University in Pennsylvania and then applied to Howard University Law School. After briefly running a law office in Baltimore devoted to handling civil rights cases for impoverished and minority clients, Marshall joined his mentor, Charles Hamilton Houston, on the NAACP legal defense team in 1936. He ultimately succeeded Houston as the NAACP's chief legal counsel.

After successfully arguing a number of graduate-school discrimination cases before the Supreme Court, Marshall took on the *Brown v. Board of Education* case. Marshall's biographers elaborate that "he was the principal architect of the strategy of using the courts to provide what the political system would not: a definition of equality that assured black Americans the full rights of citizenship."

In 1965 following an illustrious courtroom career, Marshall was appointed to the U.S. Supreme Court by President Lyndon

Johnson. Until his retirement, he established a record for supporting minority and voiceless Americans. "For much of his Supreme Court career," his biographer concludes, "as the Court's majority increasingly drew back from affirmative action and other remedies for discrimination . . . Marshall used dissenting opinions to express his disappointment and anger."

Arlington National Cemetery Website, "Thurgood Marshall: Associate Justice, United States Supreme Court," November 3, 2005. www.arlingtoncemetery.net/tmarsh.htm.

Justice Thurgood Marshall poses in judicial robes in his chambers in 1967.

Earl Warren

———————————■———————————

A native of Los Angeles, Earl Warren attended the University of California at Berkeley and its law school. Following graduation he served in the U.S. Army during World War I and then worked as a district attorney and attorney general of California before being elected governor of that state in 1942. He later played a key role in the election of President Dwight D. Eisenhower. For his record as a tough prosecutor and for his loyal Republican support, Eisenhower named Warren chief justice of the Supreme Court following the death of former chief justice Fred Vinson in 1953.

Chief Justice Earl Warren sits for a formal portrait in 1953.

Earl Warren served as chief justice during one of the most turbulent times in American history. While the most important decision during his years on the Court was the *Brown* case, Warren and the Court, from 1953 until 1969, became noted for their defense of individual rights. His law clerk, Earl Pollock, said years later that there were three things that mattered to Warren: "The first was the concept of equality; the second was education; and the third was the rights of young people to a decent life."

Quoted in David Halberstam, *The Fifties*. New York: Fawcett Columbine, 1993, p. 419.

"I Thank God I Lived to See the Day"

On Monday, May 17, 1954, Warren read the long-awaited Court decision:

> Today education is perhaps the most important function of state and local governments. . . . Today it is the principal instrument in awakening the child to cultural values, in preparing him for later professional training, and in helping him to adjust normally to his environment. In these days, it is doubtful that any child may reasonably be expected to

succeed in life if he is denied the opportunity of an education. Such an opportunity, where the state has undertaken to provide it, is a right which must be made available to all on equal terms.

We come then to the question presented: Does segregation of children in public schools solely on the basis of race . . . deprive the children of the minority group of equal educational opportunities? We believe that it does.

To separate them from others of similar age and qualifications solely because of their race generates a feeling of inferiority as to their status in the community that may affect their hearts and minds in a way unlikely ever to be undone. . . .

Standing before the U.S. Supreme Court, Thurgood Marshall (center) and other attorneys celebrate their victory in the *Brown v. Board of Education* case in 1954.

We conclude that in the field of public education the doctrine of "separate but equal" has no place. Separate educational facilities are inherently unequal. Therefore, we hold that the plaintiffs and others similarly situated for whom the actions have brought are, by reason of the segregation complained of, deprived of their equal protection of the laws guaranteed by the Fourteenth Amendment.[26]

Historians are nearly unanimous in their conviction that the *Brown* case was one of the most important decisions ever reached by the U.S. Supreme Court. The Thernstroms opine, "No legal decision in American history has had greater impact on the life of the nation, and none has provoked more controversy."[27] Historian David Halberstam agrees, writing, "*The Brown v. Board of Education* decision not only legally ended segregation, it deprived segregationist practices of their moral legitimacy as well."[28]

There was also immediate recognition across the country that this was a momentous decision. For the first time, the U.S. government was saying that segregation was wrong and must be stopped. Ninety-year-old African American civil rights leader Mary Church Terrell, upon hearing the news, spoke for many Americans—black and white—when she said, "I thank God I lived to see the day."[29]

The Southern Manifesto

While most African Americans and northern whites greeted the Supreme Court's decision with jubilation, southern whites responded with vehement criticism. Historian Weisbrot explains, "By threatening white supremacy so forthrightly, the *Brown* case intensified Southern resistance."[30] Southerners quickly dubbed the day the Court announced its ruling as "Black Monday" and swore not to abide by the decision. As an editorial in Jackson, Mississippi's newspaper proclaimed, "It [the *Brown* decision] means racial strife of the bitterest sort. Mississippi cannot and will not try to abide by such a decision."[31]

Southern politicians united in their determination to oppose the *Brown* decision and drafted what they called the Declaration

Eisenhower's Failure

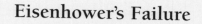

Support for and implementation of the *Brown* decision was somewhat impaired by President Dwight D. Eisenhower's silence. Eisenhower had personally hoped that the Court would uphold *Plessy* and refused to comment or associate himself with the *Brown* ruling. He had, in fact, tried to influence Chief Justice Earl Warren the night before the historic ruling. He is quoted in Stephen E. Ambrose's book *Eisenhower: Soldier and President* as commenting to Warren that southerners "are not bad people. All they are concerned about is to see that their sweet little girls are not required to sit in school alongside some big overgrown Negroes."

Eisenhower's failure to put the weight of the presidency behind the decision had wide repercussions. In the book *Civil Rights and Wrongs*, associate Supreme Court justice William O. Douglas is quoted as stating, "Ike's ominous silence on our 1954 decision gave courage to the racists who decided to resist the decision, ward by ward, precinct by precinct, town by town, county by county." Historian Ambrose agrees, writing, "Even as violence flared across the South, as the implementation of desegregation began, Eisenhower refused to ever say that he thought segregation was morally wrong. That allowed the bitter-end segregationists to claim that Ike was secretly on their side. . . . He missed a historic opportunity to provide moral leadership."

President Dwight D. Eisenhower (third from right) visits with Supreme Court justices in 1953.

Stephen E. Ambrose, *Eisenhower: Soldier and President.* New York: Touchstone, 1990, p. 367.

Harry S. Ashmore, *Civil Rights and Wrongs: A Memoir of Race and Politics: 1944–1994.* New York: Pantheon, 1994, p. 103.

of Constitutional Principles, a document that came to be referred to by historians as the Southern Manifesto. Signed by 101 out of 128 southern congressmen and senators, it declared that only state courts and government bodies—not the federal government—could rule on segregation. It condemned *Brown* as being contrary to the U.S. Constitution. The manifesto included these words: "We regard the decision of the Supreme Court in the school cases as a clear abuse of judicial power."[32]

Three southern senators took their political futures in their hands by speaking out against the manifesto and refusing to sign it. Senator Albert Gore Sr. of Tennessee said the document was "a dangerous, deceptive propaganda move which encouraged Southerners to defy the government and to disobey its laws."[33] Estes Kefauver of Tennessee, along with Lyndon B. Johnson of Texas, also refused to sign the document. Historian Brian Lamb comments on what these men risked in defying their constituents' wishes: "All but a handful of southern senators and representatives signed this manifesto because the pressure to sign built up to the point where it would have been political suicide not to sign it."[34]

Marshall, the NAACP, and African Americans across the nation reveled in the victory. All expected the federal government to act quickly to end school segregation and eagerly anticipated the desegregation of the nation's schools and the opportunities that such schools promised. Despite these hopes and high expectations, however, the end of segregation would come neither quickly nor quietly.

Chapter Three

The South's Fight Against Desegregation

While the Supreme Court had clearly stated that school segregation was unconstitutional, it did not outline how this injustice should be corrected. Nor did it set a deadline for implementation of desegregation. Concerned, in fact, that rapid action would cause a violent upheaval in the South, the justices said only that integration should be implemented gradually. The justices met late in 1954 and early in 1955 to make recommendations for how best to implement their decision.

The justices heard arguments and recommendations from the NAACP, along with those from southerners and from academicians. Suggestions ranged from immediate desegregation, while others argued for a more cautious approach, allowing the states to implement desegregation over the course of several years. In the end, caution won out, and on May 31, 1955, the Court, in a decision known as *Brown II*, asked the South to draw up desegregation plans with all deliberate speed.

The Supreme Court declared that the federal district courts in each state would, thereafter, have the jurisdiction over school desegregation cases. This meant that individuals who thought

Children in a segregated Atlanta school work on a math lesson with their teacher in 1954.

they were being forced to attend segregated schools would have to bring cases before these courts and ask them to order desegregation. Furthermore, the lower courts had no enforcement powers. It would be the job of state and local authorities to see that any court order was obeyed. Historian Harry S. Ashmore explains, "Initially, the judiciary, which had no enforcement powers of its own, had to rely on state and local authorities to carry out court orders, and most, when not openly hostile, were inhibited by the political risk involved."[35] As a result, "all deliberate speed" soon deteriorated into no speed at all as southern states either adopted a strategy of delay or simply ignored the Supreme Court altogether.

A Policy of Delay

In the months following the initial *Brown* decision, Southern resistance to desegregation made the Supreme Court's ruling virtually meaningless. Alabama governor John Patterson spoke for many southern politicians when he announced, "I will oppose with every ounce of energy I possess and will use every power at my command to prevent any mixing of white and Negro races in the classrooms of this state. . . . There can be no compromise in this fight."[36]

The first strategy adopted by many southern states was to make desegregation so difficult that only the most determined African American parents could successfully enroll their children in a previously all-white school. Between 1954 and 1958 more than four hundred laws were enacted throughout the South to delay or stop any move toward integration. Typical of such laws was one passed in Louisiana in 1956. Historian Goldfield describes it: "[Louisiana] passed a measure requiring black applicants to white public schools to present a certificate of good moral character signed by their principal and the district school superintendent before they could be admitted. The lawmakers [then] passed a companion measure providing for the dismissal of anyone signing such a certificate."[37]

The commonwealth of Virginia tried a somewhat different approach by passing laws that increased public funding of private schools. In September 1954 the governor of Virginia appointed a committee, headed by state senator Garland Gray, to examine possible responses to *Brown*. As historian Mary C. Doyle explains, the Gray Plan, released in November 1955, "called for tuition grants from public funds to aid white students attending private schools . . . a new pupil assignment plan to minimize race mixing, and an amendment to the compulsory attendance law so that no child would be required to attend an integrated school."[38]

The net effect of the southern laws was a massive delay in implementing desegregation. By 1960 fewer than 1 percent of the South's black pupils were attending desegregated schools. In South Carolina and Mississippi, not a single public school had been desegregated. "Whether accompanied by defiance and violence or by compliance and order," historian Goldfield summarizes, "school desegregation proceeded at an excruciatingly slow pace at all education levels."[39] Education experts now estimate that if this rate had been maintained it would have taken more than seven thousand years to totally desegregate the South's schools.

The White-Collar Klan

In addition to passing laws to delay desegregation, white southerners also formed a number of organizations to impede the process. The most common of these were white citizens' councils. The first such organization was formed in Mississippi, but others soon appeared in other southern states. Often called the white-collar Klan by their opponents, these groups were joined by local business owners and professionals. These councils numbered 150,000 members in the states of Alabama and Mississippi alone.

The primary method employed by the white citizens' councils was economic pressure. Historian Goldfield explains, "The councils applied systematic economic pressure on the parents of black children. . . . Composed of merchants, bankers, farmers, and politicians, these bodies controlled the economic life of the numerous small towns and cities of the Deep South."[40] Council members denied employment, credit, and public services to blacks who tried to send their children to white schools. Hundreds of blacks, for example, found their names removed from the welfare rolls, and others lost their homes when the local banks foreclosed on their mortgages. In addition, blacks lost their jobs and had their accounts closed at banks and stores throughout the South. Faced with the threat of these kinds of economic reprisals, many African Americans chose not to challenge segregation in their local schools. Historians Stephen and Abigail Thernstrom summarize that "economic pressure was more effective than running around at night wearing white sheets and burning crosses, and it was perfectly legal."[41]

Despite their pledge of nonviolent opposition to desegregation, many white citizens' councils actively encouraged violent acts by others. In fact, shortly after the *Brown* ruling, one such group circulated a handbill that was a parody of the Declaration of Independence. It read, "When in the course of human events it becomes necessary to abolish the Negro race, proper methods should be used. Among these are guns, bows and arrows, slingshots, and knives."[42] As a consequence of such incitement of violence, thousands of African American children were taunted, threatened, and attacked for trying to attend white schools. Numerous black churches, schools, and homes were burned to the ground.

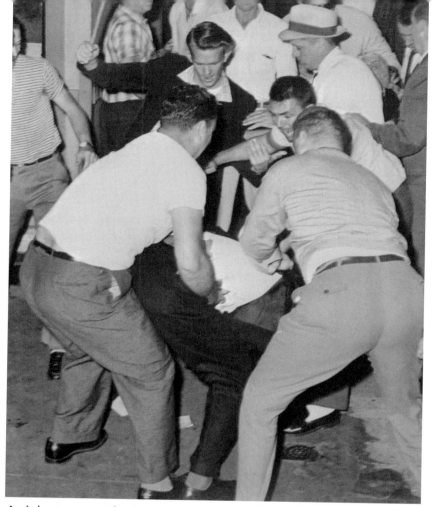

A violent group of white men opposed to integration attacks a black man in a bus station in 1961 in Birmingham, Alabama.

Southern politicians, through their words and actions, also encouraged violence. According to historians:

Political extremists received their tacit support from the refusal of elected officials to respect the law of the land, their repeated threats of interposition [taking action against any federal intervention], and their disavowal of responsibility for the violence they claimed would occur in reaction to federal efforts to enforce school desegregation.[43]

A Major Challenge

Massive resistance, delay, and violence all came into play when the first major test of the South's intention to fight school desegregation occurred in Little Rock, Arkansas, in 1957. In some ways,

Arkansas might have seemed unlikely as the site of this challenge. For one thing, a great deal of desegregation had already occurred in the state. Arkansas city buses, for instance, were already desegregated, and blacks in many parts of the state could not only vote but were being elected to public office as well. By the early 1950s, in fact, Little Rock, the capital of Arkansas, had desegregated its libraries, parks, and other public facilities.

Daisy Bates (1914–1999)

Daisy Bates, the adviser and mentor of the Little Rock teenagers, grew up in the South in the 1920s and saw racism and prejudice wherever she turned. Born in the small southern Arkansas town of Huttig, Bates attended segregated schools. She later met and married Lucius Christopher "L.C." Bates in 1941 and attended Wilberforce University in Ohio, where she studied journalism. The couple moved to Little Rock, where, in 1952, she became the president of the Arkansas branch of the NAACP. She and her husband also wrote and published a local black newspaper, the *Arkansas State Press*.

It is, however, for her role as the adviser of the Little Rock children that Daisy Bates is most remembered. Her house became the official pick-up and drop-off site for the nine youngsters as well as a gathering spot for the press. She became the children's protector and staunchest advocate, but not without repercussions. Her involvement, for instance, led to hundreds of threatening phone calls. Gunshots were fired at her house, and a burning cross was left in her yard. She and her husband also lost their foster children as a result of their active participation in the desegregation of the Little Rock school.

Later she moved to Washington, D.C., where she worked with the Democratic National Committee and in the Lyndon B. Johnson administration on the antipoverty campaign. Upon her death in 1999, Bates's coffin lay in state at the state capitol in Little Rock, an honor usually bestowed only on politicians.

In 1957 Daisy Bates stands in front of her home with four of the students who enrolled in Central High School.

In fact, compliance with the *Brown* decision had Arkansas governor Orville Faubus's complete support until late 1956. The statewide election that year, however, caused Faubus to rethink his position. The governor's opponent had charged Faubus with being soft on the desegregation issue. While Faubus won the election, his margin of victory was far less than he had anticipated. By the following spring, Faubus was reassessing his position just as the issue of desegregating Little Rock's Central High School came to the forefront.

After months of delays and appeals, the Eighth Circuit Court of Appeals in St. Louis ordered the desegregation of Central High School to proceed, beginning on September 4, 1957. A few days later the White Citizens Council of Little Rock demanded that Governor Faubus maintain the segregation of the city's schools. Fearing that he would lose the next election if he failed to take a stronger stance on the issue, Faubus announced in a fiery speech that he was sending in the Arkansas National Guard—not to protect the black students, but to keep them out of Central High. He predicted, "Blood will run in the streets if black pupils . . . enter Central High."[44]

"We Ain't Gonna Integrate"

After an attempt to enter the school on September 4, 1957, failed, the nine black teenagers who had been chosen to be the first to desegregate the school decided to wait for the district court to intervene. On September 20 federal district judge Ronald Davies ruled that Faubus's attempt to use the National Guard to keep the youngsters out was illegal. In response, Faubus removed the guard and asked the Little Rock Police Department to take charge of the situation.

The city's police officers complied, but their leaders ordered them not to intervene and put few officers on the scene. The teens, therefore, arrived to face a belligerent mob that included many white high school students. One such student, Coy Vance, aged seventeen, told a reporter, "I'm not going to school with niggers, because they are inferior to us. If I catch one, I'll chase him out of school."[45] Other students chanted: "2, 4, 6, 8, we ain't gonna integrate."[46]

Other racial epithets were hurled at the youngsters, as were rocks and rotten vegetables. In addition any black person in the

After being barred from entering Central High School by a belligerent mob, the "Little Rock Nine" form their own study group in September 1957.

vicinity became a target for violence. A pack of fifty white men, for example, chased black journalist Alex Wilson for blocks, and when they caught up to him, they hit him with fists and bricks.

When the mob learned that the black students had already entered the school through a back door, more violence broke out. The police were forced to quietly remove the black youths out of fear that the crowd would physically attack them if they left by the front doors. Historian Lamb describes what happened: "The assistant police chief, one of the great unsung heroes of our time, a man named Gene Smith, had to spirit these kids out from the basement of the school in unmarked cars with their heads down so the mob couldn't get at them."[47]

"Mob Rule Cannot Be Allowed"

From the onset of the desegregation crisis in Arkansas, President Dwight D. Eisenhower had been reluctant to speak out or commit the federal government to act. Historian David Halberstam explains his reluctance: "Conservative by nature, he saw even the smallest change in the existing racial order as radical and upsetting."[48] It took a desperate telegram from Little Rock mayor

Woodrow Wilson Mann to force the president to do something. The telegram stated, "The immediate need for federal troops is urgent. . . . Situation is out of control and police cannot disperse the mob."[49]

Based on the fact that Governor Faubus had openly violated a federal court order, Eisenhower announced that he was sending one thousand members of the U.S. Army's 101st Airborne Division to protect the students and quell the violence. In a televised address on September 24, 1957, the president stated, "Mob rule cannot be allowed to override the decisions of our courts."[50] In taking this action, Eisenhower became the first president since Ulysses S. Grant to dispatch federal troops to the South for the purpose of safeguarding African Americans.

On September 25, 1957, several army station wagons showed up at the home of Daisy Bates, the black civil rights activist who had served as the students' mentor throughout the crisis. The nine black students were escorted back to school by a handful of elite troops while hundreds of armed paratroopers stood at attention around the school's campus. Historian Halberstam explains the significance of the moment: "With the arrival of the 101st, the

In October 1957 members of the 101st Airborne Division escort African American students to a waiting car after classes at Little Rock's Central High School.

nation yet again witnessed a stunning spectacle on television: armed soldiers of one of the most honored divisions of the U.S. Army escorting young black children where once there had been a mob."[51]

Segregationists throughout the South were outraged at Eisenhower's actions. Most perceived the presence of federal troops as an invasion. In Marshall, Texas, a speaker at a meeting of a local civic club proclaimed that the deployment of troops was the darkest day in the South since the Civil War. Throughout the South, newspaper editors launched a chorus of outrage. And Faubus himself protested loudly the federal government's encroachment of state rights, claiming that Arkansas was now an occupied territory.

The Black Experience

The violence and harassment of the black students, however, did not end with their admittance to the formerly all-white school. Historian Halberstam describes what happened in Little Rock, events that were repeated across the South: "Inside the school, there was a systematic and extremely well-organized assault upon the . . . children by high school age segregationists."[52] These kinds of actions were aimed not just at the black students but at any white student who showed any sign of friendliness to them.

The attacks took the form of kicking, hitting, and tripping. In addition, white students hurled verbal racial epithets at the black students as they walked down the halls. African American students had their books stolen, their hair pulled, their clothing ripped, and their lockers vandalized and painted with vicious racial slurs. In Little Rock, white students poured hot soup on their black counterparts in the cafeteria, and others threw firecrackers and even dynamite sticks.

One of the worst acts of violence was perpetrated against Melba Pattillo at Central High School when a white student sprayed acid into her eyes. Pattillo was also cornered and choked by a group of white football players. In her autobiography, *Warriors Don't Cry*, Pattillo summarizes her experiences at Little Rock: "In 1957, while most teenage girls were listening to Buddy Holly's *Peggy Sue*, watching Elvis gyrate, and collecting crinoline slips, I was escaping the hanging rope of a lynch mob, dodging

The Importance of the Media to Desegregation

The advent of television is often credited with bringing the civil rights movement into the homes of millions of Americans and helping to garner support for its goals and objectives.

The image of a lone black girl facing the mob in Little Rock shocked the nation. Elizabeth Eckford had not received the message that she should meet the other children at the home of their mentor, Daisy Bates, so she ventured alone into the crowd. Photographers and reporters captured her picture and her story for the nation and the world to see. Unlike other racial crises of the past, this one was captured on film and shown on the new media of television. Millions of people were able to follow the events in Arkansas from their living rooms. Shock waves reverberated across America as viewers watched and listened to the violence unfold.

They watched as Eckford approached the schoolhouse door only to have an Arkansas National Guardsman, under orders from Governor Orville Faubus, raise his bayonet and bar her way inside. Viewers listened as the angry mob shouted racial epithets and threatened to kill her. In Sanford Wexler's history of the civil rights movement, Eckford recounts what happened: "I tried to see a friendly face somewhere in the mob. . . . I looked into the face of an old woman, and it seemed a kind face, but when I looked at her again, she spat on me." William Doyle, in his book *An American Insurrection*, writes that the young girl eventually found comfort from Benjamin Fine, a reporter from the *New York Times*, who wrapped his arms around her and whispered, "Don't let them see you cry."

Sanford Wexler, *The Civil Rights Movement.* New York: Facts On File, 1993, p. 89.

William Doyle, *An American Insurrection: The Battle of Oxford, Mississippi: 1962.* New York: Doubleday, 2001, p. 7.

lighted sticks of dynamite, and washing away burning acid sprayed into my eyes."[53]

A few white students were at least willing to give integration a chance to work. One anonymous Central High student stated, "It's the parents who cause all this trouble. . . . We don't know if we like integration. Let us try it. Make the parents go home."[54] Many other students felt the same way, saying that if their parents had allowed the students themselves to deal with the situation the entire crisis might have been avoided. And on at least one occasion, when a group of white students saw one of the black youths sitting alone at lunchtime, they invited him to join them. Such acts of tolerance, however, were few and far between.

The army troops were withdrawn in November 1957, and the Arkansas National Guard was given the responsibility of protecting the students. The guard remained on the school premises the entire school year. Harassment and violence continued in Little

Freedom-of-Choice Plans

---■---

One of the methods by which southerners hoped to forestall school desegregation was the creation of so-called freedom-of-choice plans. These plans allowed students to choose their own schools. They also required black parents to request admission to white schools on an individual basis. In his book *Civil Rights and Wrongs*, historian Harry S. Ashmore explains, "The resulting freedom of choice policy provided that any qualified black petitioner must be admitted to a white school if there were a vacancy in an appropriate classroom, but in the absence of such a demand, segregation would be considered voluntary." In practice, however, black children found that they faced lengthy application procedures, intimidating interviews, and high rates of rejection. The plan clearly favored white children, and it was assumed that no white student would voluntarily choose to attend a black school.

In 1968 the U.S. Supreme Court gave its ruling in a Virginia case, *Green v. New Kent County School Board*. In his book *Black, White, and Southern*, historian David R. Goldfield quotes the decision as stating that "the so-called freedom of choice plans allowing limited numbers of blacks to attend white schools were no longer appropriate means of complying with the *Brown* decision." As a result of this decision, quotas and statistics were used as a basis for school populations. Schools that were mostly black were thus considered educationally inferior and constitutionally suspect.

Harry S. Ashmore, *Civil Rights and Wrongs: A Memoir of Race and Politics: 1944–1994.* New York: Pantheon, 1994, p. 154.

David R. Goldfield, *Black, White, and Southern: Race Relations and Southern Culture, 1940 to the Present.* Baton Rouge: Louisiana State University Press, 1990, p. 257.

Rock for several years, but that did not prevent the integration of the other high schools in the city. All but one of the nine teenagers eventually graduated from Central High School; the ninth student transferred to a school out of state.

School Closures

After the federal intervention in the Little Rock crisis, southern politicians there and elsewhere realized that simply refusing to follow court orders could slow down the process but not prevent desegregation. These leaders sought other means to preserve the old ways. In 1958, for instance, Governor Faubus pushed a bill through the Arkansas legislature that gave him the power to temporarily close Little Rock's schools, an action that could become permanent with voter approval. Little Rock's white residents supported the governor's decision by a 19,470 to 7,561 vote, closing the schools for the entire year of 1959. In Virginia, Governor J. Lindsay Almond took similar steps, shutting down the schools in Norfolk rather than agreeing to desegregation. The schools there stayed shut for five months before the NAACP sued and the courts ordered them reopened.

Thousands of students, black and white, were affected by the closure of schools throughout the South. "Today [in Arkansas]," according to the *Arkansas Gazette*, "class members [still] recall being caught in the middle, victimized by a situation out of their control."[55] In fact, members of these so-called lost classes use words such as *horrible, traumatic*, and *tragic* to describe the school closings. Thousands of students, black and white, were forced to leave home and live with relatives in neighboring states so they could continue their education. One such student, Ritgerod Rhodes, was told by her mother to pack her belongings so her father could take her to live with her grandparents in Missouri. She remembers, "I cried all the way."[56] Other students had difficulty adjusting to school in distant locales, where they were questioned about their role in the desegregation crisis. Don Smith, president of the student council in Little Rock's Hall High School, recalls, "I was some kind of curiosity."[57] Most white students managed to attend school somewhere and were ultimately able to graduate. African American youngsters, however, had few if any options; thousands of them had virtually no education for years.

The students who defied segregation in 1957, the "Little Rock Nine," share a joke after posing for photos on the grounds of Central High School in 1997.

In many areas, southerners who could afford to do so responded to the school closures by establishing private academies, which, because they received no public funding, were allowed to discriminate as much as they cared to. Many localities tried to support these schools by a variety of schemes. Initially, for instance, the Little Rock School Board tried leasing its school buildings to a private corporation that would then run the schools as private academies open only to white students. Ultimately, this tactic failed when public funding of private schools was ruled unconstitutional. With no alternative left, many localities reopened their schools.

Economic and Political Realities

Indeed, a combination of political and economic realities finally forced many southern cities and towns to desegregate their schools. New Orleans was a notable example of this phenomenon. In the fall of 1960 after a lawsuit by a group of black parents had resulted in a court order to desegregate, violence erupted. Local politician Leander Perez used racial slurs as he incited the crowd: "Don't wait until the burr-heads are forced into your schools. Do something about it now!"[58] The next day three thousand whites rioted through the downtown area, throwing bottles and stones at passing blacks. Frightened by the violence, northern tourists, who had long been a mainstay of the city's economy, began staying away. By the end of December, white business owners were calling for desegregation in order to entice the tourists back to New Orleans.

In the end it was another financial consideration—federal funding of many school programs—that forced most school districts to desegregate. Of prime importance was the passage of the Civil Rights Act of 1964. Historians John Hope Franklin and Alfred A. Moss Jr. elaborate on how the new law worked to promote school desegregation: "Since the Act barred discrimination in federally aided projects and programs, school districts receiving federal funds were required to desegregate or to present acceptable plans for desegregating their schools."[59] This meant that if a school district failed to desegregate quickly or at least present a plan that had a chance of working, the federal government could withhold all the money it would ordinarily have provided for such things as equipment, books, and various special programs. As a result of this sort of pressure, by September 1965 all but 124 of southern and border state school districts had presented to federal authorities acceptable plans for desegregating.

While political and economic factors played a role in ending school desegregation in the South, more than forty years later American politicians say that the black youngsters themselves deserve much of the credit. Day after day African American students endured intimidating and often physically dangerous confrontations as they attended formerly all-white schools. In 1999 the Little Rock Nine, the African American men and women who, as teenagers, had faced down the Arkansas mob, received some of the recognition they deserved. In a ceremony at the White House, then-president Bill Clinton awarded them with the nation's highest civilian honor, the Congressional Gold Medal. They accepted the medal on behalf of the thousands of other African American children who had challenged school segregation and succeeded.

At the ceremony honoring the Little Rock students, Senator Tim Hutchinson of Arkansas stated:

We salute you nine brave souls who helped bring down the wall of hatred, misunderstanding, and prejudice. . . . They quietly but resolutely persevered, and their courage forced the nation to come to terms with the incongruity of revering the Declaration of Independence while simultaneously denying the fundamental truth that all men are created equal.[60]

Chapter Four

The North: De Facto Segregation

With desegregation finally proceeding in the South, the eyes of the government and the courts turned northward. Initially, it was generally agreed by politicians and the courts that the *Brown* decision did not apply in the North since there were no laws there that specifically prohibited blacks and whites from attending the same schools. Despite this fact, however, northern and western schools were often just as segregated as those in the South. For instance, in the school year of 1972–1973, only about one-fourth of black children in these areas of the country were enrolled in schools that had a white majority. Such de facto segregation, sociologists and government policy makers contended, needed to be eliminated.

The primary cause of de facto segregation was the rigid racial patterns in residential neighborhoods. There was tremendous economic growth following the end of World War II, and many industrial and manufacturing companies expanded. Needing more space, such firms often moved from inner-city areas to the growing suburbs. With an economic upswing, more and more Americans were employed and able to afford better housing. They often followed industry in the relocation to suburban areas. Purchases of new homes skyrocketed. Long discriminated against in hiring for better-paying jobs, most African Americans simply could not afford to buy homes in these newly created suburbs.

In addition, suburban governments often used a variety of techniques to prohibit blacks from moving into new neighborhoods. As each residential development was created, homeowners were advised that their lots needed to be specific sizes and that their homes must be a certain number of square feet in size. The cost of these requirements was often prohibitive for black families. Real estate agents also steered their African American clients away from white neighborhoods to all-black

Young whites protest integrated neighborhoods in 1967 in Milwaukee. One sign bears a threatening message for James Groppi, a leader in the city's integration movement.

areas. Additionally, banks routinely refused to issue mortgages to black applicants, effectively keeping many suburban neighborhoods all white.

The population of schools, which drew on nearby neighborhoods for their students, reflected this housing pattern, resulting in black schools in the inner cities and white schools in the suburbs. Historians Stephen and Abigail Thernstrom summarize, "A neighborhood school system plus residential segregation was a

De Facto Segregation in Milwaukee

While no laws in Milwaukee, Wisconsin, specified segregated schools, students in that city were nonetheless attending such schools. The majority of African Americans lived in the poorest area of the city because of poverty. With the majority of whites living in the suburbs, most of the inner-city schools were over 95 percent black. Many suburban schools had no black students at all. To make matters worse, the black schools were clearly inferior in all aspects.

In 1963 a local attorney and president of the Wisconsin NAACP charged that Milwaukee was guilty of de facto segregation. Superintendent of schools Angus Rothwell ordered an immediate investigation of the charges. The resultant report showed that the schools were, in fact, heavily segregated and that the school board was doing nothing to alleviate the problem. Despite suggestions and orders from the superintendent to desegregate, the Milwaukee school board refused to change anything.

This provoked the NAACP and the newly created Milwaukee United School Integration Committee to organize a boycott of white businesses in the hopes of impacting the economic well-being of the area and forcing changes in the school system. After that attempt failed, the group brought a lawsuit against the school district and won. Despite this victory, the Milwaukee school board delayed implementing desegregation until 1976, thirteen years later. At that time there was only a 21 percent white presence in minority schools. Ten years later the figure had risen by 10 percent.

formula that added up to schools that were racially imbalanced and, thus, segregated de facto."[61]

A Major Challenge

In the South de facto segregation proved just as difficult to erad-icate as de jure—that is, law-based—segregation had. For exam-ple, during the 1968–1969 school year, Charlotte in Mecklen-burg County, North Carolina, had a total of more than eighty thousand students attending more than one hundred different schools. While desegregation had been proceeding for several years in this community, the schools were still racially imbal-anced. Nearly one-fourth of Charlotte's students were black, for instance, and nearly all of them attended all-black segregated schools.

Once again, it took court intervention to correct the problem. In 1968 parent James E. Swann challenged the de facto segrega-tion that was present in the city. District court judge James B. McMillan responded to Swann's challenge by appointing a panel of experts to investigate the situation and submit a plan for achieving true desegregation.

In the end McMillan created his own plan. To correct the problem of racially segregated neighborhoods, he set a quota of 71 percent white and 29 percent black for each school, a figure that roughly corresponded to the overall racial breakdown of the entire area. Since achieving this goal would require some stu-dents to attend schools that were not close to home, McMillan recommended that the school board make buses available.

The school board and residents of Charlotte vehemently protested the decision. Not happy with the thought of their chil-dren being transported by bus to distant school districts, parents petitioned the school board to delay the busing order. Thousands of parents and other concerned citizens staged protests and demonstrations to delay the onset of the busing decision. Amidst these continued protests, arguments, delays, and challenges, the case was ultimately appealed to the U.S. Supreme Court.

Swann v. Charlotte-Mecklenburg

In 1971, after hearing the arguments in *Swann v. Charlotte-Mecklenburg*, the Supreme Court unanimously agreed that whatever

African American boys talk in front of an integrated school bus in Berkeley, California, in 1971, the year court-ordered busing took effect.

steps were necessary to achieve desegregation should be taken. Chief Justice Warren Burger spoke for the Court in stating:

> Nearly 17 years ago this Court held, in explicit terms, that state-imposed segregation by race in public schools denies equal protection of the laws. At no time has the Court deviated in the slightest degree from that holding or its constitutional underpinnings. . . . The burden on a school board today is to come forward with a plan that promises realistically to work. . . . The objective in dealing with the issues presented . . . is to see that school authorities exclude no pupil of a racial minority of any school, directly or indirectly, on account of race.[62]

Burger went on to explain that school segregation was wrong, no matter what the contributing factors were. He concluded that whatever measures that were needed to correct the problem must be initiated immediately. This included busing for the purposes of desegregating the public schools.

School busing had long been an accepted part of American education. In fact, prior to the *Swann* case buses transported more than 9 million schoolchildren—nearly half of all students—to and from school each day. Now, however, parents objected. In part these objections were based on long-held dislike of federal involvement in education. "Once school transportation and civil rights were paired [however]," opines historian Weisbrot, "public approval of busing plummeted and neighborhoods began tensing against a federally imposed presence."[63]

The Changing Definition of Desegregation

As the formula of using population statistics and racial quotas along with busing to achieve desegregation was put into effect in city after city throughout the country, the definition of desegregation gradually changed. The Civil Rights Act of 1964 had clearly stated that desegregation did not necessarily mean that schools had to be racially balanced. The Civil Rights Act had, instead, simply stated that race could not be used in determining the assignment of students to buildings in public school systems. This meant that if an African American child applied to a formerly all-white school, the child's admission could not be denied simply because he or she was black. By the same token, if no black child applied, the school was not required to take any further steps to enroll black students. This understanding began to change in the late 1960s and early 1970s.

In the 1970s the U.S. Supreme Court further expanded its definition of segregation to include any action by public authorities that might contribute to a racial imbalance in the schools. The Court also urged the active integration of African American students into previously white schools. Desegregation had simply meant the end of segregation and discrimination, while integration meant including blacks at white schools according to some kind of racial formula. This was new. For many years after *Brown*, the common understanding was that there was no violation of the Constitution if the races were separated by such things as residential patterns or poverty. By the mid-1960s, however, the emphasis shifted to the mixing of the races in schools in proportions that matched local populations.

As the definition of desegregation changed, the attention of the courts moved north. One of the first northern cases involving this new objective to reach the Court was *Keyes v. School District Number 1*, which involved racially imbalanced schools in Denver, Colorado. Although Denver had never had any laws requiring racial separation, some of the city's schools were, for all practical purposes, segregated. The local school board claimed this was due to voluntary residential patterns. "The lower court [however]," according to the Thernstroms, "had found intentional segregation in the subtle steps taken to confine black students living in one section of the city to predominantly black schools."[64] The Supreme Court agreed and recommended extensive busing to correct the racial imbalance.

White Flight

As large, primarily urban school systems responded to de facto segregation by busing students, some white parents elected to simply move out to surrounding suburbs that were not subject to the court orders. This, some social historians say, contributed to "white flight." The Thernstroms define this phenomenon as "the familiar term for the shift of students from urban school systems to suburban or private schools in response to court ordered . . . [desegregation or] busing schemes."[65] The effect on the racial composition of many school districts was noticeable. "As a rule of thumb," one historian says, "districts that were subject to court-ordered integration lost about fifty percent of their white students within ten years."[66]

White flight became a stark reality, for instance, in Boston's city schools, where the percentage of white students dropped from nearly 50 percent to less than 10 percent over a period of twenty years after the court-ordered desegregation of the schools began. During the latter part of the 1970s more than twenty thousand white students in Boston alone quit public school and enrolled in parochial schools, private academies, and schools in other cities. In 1970 sixty-two thousand white students were attending public city schools; by 1994 this number had dropped to eleven thousand.

White students and parents take to the streets of Boston in 1974 to protest school integration by forced busing.

A Recipe for Violence

Boston, like many other northern cities, had segregated school systems primarily because of housing patterns. "Because students were assigned to schools based on where they lived, schools in primarily white areas such as South Boston and Charlestown had a mostly white student body," historians explain, "while schools in black areas such as Roxbury were overwhelmingly black."[67]

Faced with desegregating and integrating their own school systems, some northerners responded with a vehemence reminiscent of what was seen in Little Rock, Arkansas. Boston's experience was particularly shocking for northerners who had bitterly condemned southerners for opposing desegregation. Historian Grace Elizabeth Hale summarizes, "Northern whites often resisted . . . as massively as had white Southerners."[68]

On June 21, 1974, Judge W. Arthur Garrity ruled that de facto segregation did exist in Boston and that it must be corrected. He then announced that the schools in Roxbury would be combined with those of South Boston to achieve integration. The Boston School Board implemented Garrity's plan in September 1974.

A 1975 demonstration in Boston turns violent as some youths throw rocks and use baseball bats against supporters of school busing.

As had happened in the South, violence erupted over the desegregation plan. In South Boston, white protesters threw rocks at buses carrying black students, shouted racial epithets, and hurled eggs and tomatoes at the students themselves. Ellen Jackson, who ran a community center in Roxbury, described the scene as a busload of black elementary schoolchildren returned home: "When the kids came, everybody just broke out in tears and started crying. . . . They had glass in their hair. They were scared."[69]

The effect of such tension on the school environment was anything but positive. Phyliss Ellison, a student at South Boston High School, commented about the violence that erupted: "On a normal day, there would be anywhere between ten and fifteen fights. . . . You can't imagine how tense it was in the classroom. . . . The black students sat on one side of the classes. The white students sat on the other side."[70] Racial tensions continued to mount throughout the school year. In South Boston, the schools had to be closed frequently and required detachments of state troopers and police to be on campus to keep order. The specter of violence would continue to haunt South Boston High School, and as late as 1999, Boston police were still patrolling the grounds of the school.

The Response to Busing

The response to court-ordered busing varied from community to community. It was met with violence in Charlotte, Boston, and other cities, but it was achieved elsewhere without fanfare or protest. In 1968 for instance, Berkeley, California, became the first American city to achieve full integration through the use of cross-town busing. It was accomplished there with little violence or opposition of any sort.

A few communities took creative steps to ensure the success of busing. In Lexington, Massachusetts, for example, the school system developed a program under which host families helped bused students find acceptance in their new schools. Under this plan, each black student spent time with a white family in the community. According to both the white and black students who participated, this program helped promote a sense of community. It also enabled students of both races to build lasting friendships with each other.

Violence Erupts in Michigan

On a hot night in August 1971, just a few days before the start of school, ten school buses exploded in Pontiac, Michigan. The explosion came after nearly two years of conflict centered around the impending integration of Pontiac's schools through the use of busing. An unnamed local official commented on the violence at the time: "I'm frankly ashamed to say . . . that I am a citizen of this city!"

Despite laws forbidding residential housing segregation, the city's neighborhoods and schools were racially segregated. To alleviate the problem, a federal judge ordered Pontiac's school board to bus pupils in order to achieve integration. Opponents of the plan immediately initiated efforts to block the plan. White parents kept their children home from school, staged sit-in demonstrations along the bus routes, and sent their children to private and parochial schools in large numbers. Violence also broke out between black and white students on a near-daily basis. A lawyer for the white parents stated, "I can't in good conscience tell parents . . . to send their children to school where friction is so great that they're going to the hospital day after day."

The white parents, who belonged to the National Action Group (a local homeowners' group with more than twenty thousand supporters), later continued their opposition by staging a forty-four-day march from Pontiac to Washington, D.C. The group hoped to pressure congressional leaders to vote against busing. Their march and protest, however, failed to change the law, and the buses continued to roll in Pontiac.

Quoted in Patricia Zacharias, "Irene McCabe and Her Battle Against Busing," *Detroit News.* http://info.detnews.com/history/story/index.cfm?id=161& category=people.

Those who actually attended the newly integrated schools later recalled a wide range of reactions among the students themselves. Many students reported that desegregation helped foster at least some interracial understanding. Bostonian Katani Sumner describes her experience with the integrated school system there:

I was really fearful of white people. . . . And I remember . . . after attending school there for a while and thinking, "Wow, there are nice white people." My [previous] exposure to white people were those on television . . . and I hadn't had much interaction with them. So if . . . for no other reason, it changed my perspective on people in general. . . . "They do things just like we do."[71]

"It Was the Worst Experience of My Life"

Many black students recalled that they found integration disconcerting. Kevin Merida, now a columnist for the *Washington Post*, was one of thousands of African American children bused in Maryland's Prince George County in the 1970s. He states, "It was taking us out of our comfort zone. Our whole routine changed . . . you felt sort of like an experiment. . . . We kind of felt like often we were under inspection. Teachers didn't know what to make of us. . . . There were a lot of difficult moments."[72]

Another former student discussed her experience on a radio call-in show, noting the sense of being unwanted:

I was bused in 1959 from my completely black grade school to a completely white grade school in South St. Louis City. . . . It was the worst experience of my life. I was taken out of everything that was familiar and plopped into a school and an environment that did not want us, that were very hostile. We had separate recess. We had separate eating times . . . we were put in two rooms in the basement of the building.[73]

As opposition to busing as a tool for integration grew, some politicians seized on it as an opportunity to broaden their base of support. President Richard Nixon was among the many leading politicians who spoke out against busing. Nixon later went so far as to hint that he would try to have any federal officials who promoted busing fired. In 1971, after the *Swann* decision, Nixon went on television and spoke to the nation: "Busing kids across a city to an inferior school just to meet some social planner's concept of what is considered to be the correct racial balance [is wrong.]"[74]

"Not Guilty of Segregative Practices"

As whites continued to flee to the suburbs, achieving racial balance in some locales became increasingly difficult. Detroit, Michigan, was just one example. There, the jagged outlines of the Detroit school district abutted other, largely white—and less populous—districts. In the early 1970s, historian Carl T. Rowan explains, "Black children in overcrowded schools were transported past white schools with vacancies to distant schools that were predominantly black."[75] After finding the school board guilty of intentional discrimination, a federal district judge ordered a merger of the city's predominantly black school district with Detroit's many white suburban school districts. The plan required the busing of more than three hundred thousand children.

This plan was challenged by Michigan governor William Milliken. This case, *Milliken v. Bradley*, ultimately went to the U.S. Supreme Court, where the justices overturned the district court's decision in a five-to-four decision. On July 25, 1974, the Court announced that "the trial record had not demonstrated that the suburban communities were themselves guilty of segregative practices, or that any actions taken by the suburbs were responsible for the racial mix in the Detroit schools."[76] Essentially the Court had ruled that because the suburbs had not caused the racial imbalance, they were under no obligation to participate in correcting the problem.

Busing and integration remained controversial issues, receiving support in some communities and violent opposition in others. Regardless of whether a person supported or opposed it, however, busing and the establishment of racial quotas did help end segregation in many areas of the United States. Most historians, sociologists, and educators contend, in fact, that desegregation would have been impossible to achieve without busing in many areas of the country.

Chapter Five

Breaking the Color Barrier on College Campuses

For several years following the *Brown* decision in 1954, the nation's attention was largely focused on segregation in the country's elementary and high schools. Little attention was paid to the discrimination that existed on college campuses. Segregation had long existed at the university level in the South. Prior to the last half of the twentieth century, those African Americans who desired a college education were forced to attend all-black institutions, which were traditionally underfunded and controlled by white administrators. This often prevented the schools from providing a quality education to black students. Historian Litwack explains, "Under steady scrutiny by white[s] . . . black schools and colleges found it impossible to fulfill the vast array of expectations imposed upon them."[77]

Many northern universities, on the other hand, had been accepting qualified African American applicants for more than one hundred years. Hundreds of enterprising black graduates had gone on to establish themselves in many professional fields. Despite their success, however, the number of blacks who attended northern universities with diverse student bodies was low when compared with those who attended all-black ones.

Early Attempts to Desegregate

The first attempt to challenge segregation on college campuses in the South looked as though it might proceed without serious opposition. In February 1956 an African American woman named Autherine Lucy was admitted to the University of Alabama. She was twenty-six years old, already had a bachelor's

Accompanied by a police escort in 1956, Autherine Lucy becomes the first black student accepted at the University of Alabama.

degree from all-black Selma University, and was hoping to obtain her master's degree at Alabama. Arriving on campus, however, Lucy was met by a mob of screaming whites who threw eggs at her and blocked her from entering the administration building. After a cross was burned on the college lawn, fears arose that the Ku Klux Klan, the violent white supremacist organization who used burning crosses to terrorize black southerners, would harm her. After that incident, a police escort saw to it that she got to class safely.

Waving Confederate flags, a rioting mob of white students at the University of Alabama protests the enrollment of Autherine Lucy.

Shortly after the semester started, the university suspended Lucy. Historians Stephen and Abigail Thernstrom explain the college's reasoning: "The University suspended her on the grounds that her presence on campus would provoke further mob action."[78] She was ultimately reinstated, then expelled, and reinstated again. By this time the stress of being a constant target of racism caused Lucy's health to deteriorate, and she decided to withdraw from school. It would not be until thirty years later, in 1992, that Lucy received a letter from the University of Alabama, informing her that she had been readmitted to the university. She finally obtained her long overdue degree on the same day her daughter received hers.

Not every southern university fought integration, however. A few years later the University of Georgia desegregated its campus by allowing the admission of two African American students, Charlayne Hunter and Hamilton Holmes. These two students were admitted without mob action and violence. Both students graduated from Georgia; Hunter later became a television journalist, and Holmes became the first black graduate of Emory Medical School. Hunter later commented on the meaning of her achievement: "It would be the last time that whites could demand of me or any other Black person . . . that we . . . accept the secondary and inferior role they had consigned to us."[79]

A few other southern universities also did not oppose efforts by African Americans to enter undergraduate and graduate programs. Most of the South's institutions of higher learning, however, took steps to segregate the black students. At the University of Arkansas, for instance, a young black man in the law school was forced to sit in class surrounded by a white picket fence. Other students faced similar humiliating reminders that whites felt they did not belong. It would take a number of significant challenges before African Americans in any number would be allowed to enter predominantly white institutions of higher learning.

Breaking the White Monopoly

Little attention had been paid nationally to the efforts of Lucy, Hunter, Holmes, and others during their admissions to previously segregated universities. That changed in 1962 when James

At the University of Mississippi, James Meredith registers for classes in 1962 as U.S. marshals stand guard on the campus.

Meredith applied for admission to the University of Mississippi. Largely as a result of the new communication medium of television, hundreds of thousands of Americans followed the course of events that took place in the university town of Oxford, Mississippi.

While in the U.S. Air Force, Meredith had taken college courses and had also briefly attended Mississipi's all-black state-supported college, Jackson State University. During the spring of 1961 Meredith decided to transfer his credits to the University of

Mississippi and submitted the necessary paperwork for the fall semester. When school officials learned that he was African American, however, they rejected his application.

Meredith wrote to Thurgood Marshall, who had successfully argued *Brown v. Board of Education*, asking for his assistance: "My long preserved ambition has been to break the monopoly on rights and privileges held by the whites of the state of Mississippi."[80] Marshall encouraged Meredith to pursue his ambitions, following which Meredith hired a lawyer in order to file a lawsuit to gain admission. It took a fifteen-month legal battle and several court rejections before the Fifth Judicial Court in September 1962 ordered the university to admit him. When the university still balked, the case was heard before the U.S. Supreme Court. Historian Robert Dallek summarizes, "Supported by the NAACP in a series of court contests, Meredith won an appeal to the United States Supreme Court on September 10, 1962. . . . [The Court ordered] the university to end its calculated campaign of delay, harassment, and masterly inactivity, and admit him."[81]

When word of Meredith's application became public, Mississippi politicians and citizens reacted vehemently and violently. They vowed that no black would ever enter the University of Mississippi. The state's governor, Ross Barnett, adamantly voiced his opposition in an address to his constituents: "No school will be integrated while I am your governor."[82] Barnett further vowed his determination in a speech on September 13, 1962: "There is no case in history where the Christian race has survived social integration. . . . We must either submit to the unlawful dictate of the federal government or stand up like men and tell them never."[83]

"The Appearance of a Battlefield"

On Sunday, September 30, 1962, the day before Meredith was supposed to start classes, tensions began to mount on the campus and throughout the small town of Oxford. Anticipating violence, President John F. Kennedy dispatched five hundred federal marshals to protect Meredith. Despite the marshals' presence, by the time Meredith appeared more than two thousand protesters filled the campus. An anonymous Mississippi policeman expressed the dominant sentiment of the mob when he stated, "I don't give a damn whether they got U.S. Marshals or not. That

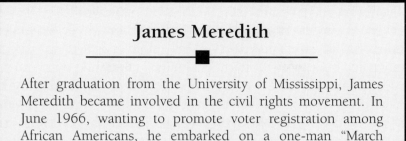

James Meredith

After graduation from the University of Mississippi, James Meredith became involved in the civil rights movement. In June 1966, wanting to promote voter registration among African Americans, he embarked on a one-man "March Against Fear." His plan was to walk from Memphis, Tennessee, to Jackson, Mississippi. He hoped to show that if he could walk alone and unharmed through the state of Mississippi that his fellow blacks could vote without fear of violence and harassment. He had only walked 20 miles (32km) when his journey came to an abrupt stop.

Historian David R. Goldfield writes about what happened: "A shot crackled through the stillness of a late spring morning, and Meredith fell, wounded by buck shot." The assailant was a thirty-year-old Ku Klux Klansman who, though he confessed to the shooting on the spot, was neither handcuffed by the police nor severely punished. Martin Luther King Jr., along with other notable civil rights figures, later completed the march Meredith had started.

David R. Goldfield, *Black, White and Southern: Race Relations and Southern Culture, 1940 to the Present.* Baton Rouge: Louisiana State University Press, 1990, p. 223.

James Meredith lies on the ground in 1966 after being shot during his march in Mississippi.

nigger ain't going to Mississippi University—period."[84]

Violence soon erupted between the mob and the federal marshals. Within hours members of the mob had occupied many university buildings. Molotov cocktails—makeshift bombs consisting of bottles filled with gasoline and stoppered with a lighted bit of cloth—were thrown. Nearby cars and homes were vandalized and burned. No one was safe: Dozens of reporters and photographers were beaten by members of the mob, and the marshals were hit with birdshot fired from shotguns. Rioters also harassed and attacked hundreds of African Americans who were reporting to work at the university. Oxford mayor Richard Elliott later reported, "There were a number of highway patrolmen standing there just watching the attack [on black workers.]"[85] Under orders from the governor not to intervene, many state troopers stood laughing as African American workers were assaulted.

Though outnumbered, the federal marshals stood their ground throughout the night. Although they carried firearms loaded with live ammunition, they never fired their rifles. They relied instead on tear gas and billy clubs to hold back the mob. There was no end in sight to the violence until the arrival of five thousand U.S. Army troops from Fort Bragg, North Carolina, dispatched to Oxford by President Kennedy to lend support to the federal marshals. By the time the soldiers helped quell the violence and disperse the mob, 160 federal marshals had been wounded, 28 of them by gunfire. Two people had been killed: a French newsman and a local repairman. Claude Sitton, a journalist, later reported, "The tree-dotted mall had the appearance of a battlefield."[86]

Images from the night of violence in Oxford showed up on television the next night. Americans were shocked at what they witnessed.

Harassed and Victimized

On October 1, 1962, James Meredith finally attended his first class at the University of Mississippi. The university's other students made life miserable for Meredith. Despite being always accompanied by soldiers, Meredith was harassed and victimized throughout his year at the Ole Miss campus. On returning to the

In 1963 Vivian Malone registers at the University of Alabama, where Governor George Wallace tried to prevent her from integrating the school.

dorm one afternoon, for example, Meredith discovered a life-size effigy of himself hanging from the window in his room with a noose around its neck. This was particularly terrifying because of the long history of lynching used by the Ku Klux Klan as a weapon against African Americans. Despite the continued intimidation and threats, Meredith graduated from the university in 1964 with a bachelor's degree in political science.

In June 1963 a second-black student, Cleveland McDowell, followed Meredith's example and enrolled at the university's law school. In contrast to Meredith, McDowell enrolled without incident. It would, however, be nearly ten years before African Americans were accepted in large numbers. As a result of continuous pressure from the African American community, the University of Mississippi eventually responded to steady black enrollment by creating an Afro-American studies department in 1970 and by opening a black fraternity in 1988. Today the university is more than 10 percent black. Visitors to the Ole Miss Campus, however, can still see the bullet holes on many of the school's buildings.

"Segregation Forever!"

In the wake of the desegregation of the University of Mississippi, the integration of other southern colleges proceeded, but unevenly. Some institutions, such as Clemson University in South Carolina, quietly desegregated. Officials at these institutions had seen the violence that the presence of federal troops could provoke and opted instead to encourage compliance with the law. Still, there were cases in which state officials chose to resist. Governor George Wallace of Alabama, when faced with integrating the all-white University of Alabama, chose instead to defy the federal government.

Wallace's resistance was planned for the maximum dramatic effect. Two African American students—Vivian Malone and James Hood—had gone through the process of being accepted to the University of Alabama. Governor Wallace, however, was waiting at the registration desk when the two arrived to sign up for classes. He drew a chalk line on the floor and stated unequivocally that, as long as he was governor, no black student would get past it.

On the morning of June 11, 1963, Wallace was on campus to greet Assistant U.S. Attorney General Nicholas Katzenbach, who was under orders from President Kennedy to make sure the students were admitted. Katzenbach handed Wallace an order from the president that he step aside and allow the students to enroll. Wallace read the order and stated he would never obey it. He then walked away, and the students were admitted. His defiant stance, however, had made Wallace a hero to white supremacists. Many southerners ardently supported Wallace for his vow, uttered in his inauguration speech of January 1963: "Segregation now—segregation tomorrow—segregation forever!"[87] Once

George Wallace (1919–1998)

George Corley Wallace, the Alabama governor who tried to block the admittance of blacks to the University of Alabama, is best known for his racist stance during that and similar altercations. A lawyer by trade, Wallace had run for governor in 1958 and had been defeated partly because of his anti–Ku Klux Klan stance. After that loss, he adopted a hard-line segregationist viewpoint and won the governor's seat in the next election.

Wallace came into the national spotlight in 1963, when he stood in front of the University of Alabama offices and attempted to stop the desegregation of that school. A year later Wallace mounted his first presidential campaign. Using his support of states' rights and his colorful and energetic rhetoric, he won widespread national appeal. He ran again in 1968 and garnered enough votes, many political analysts agree, to affect the presidential outcome. During his campaign in Maryland on May 15, 1972, Wallace was shot four times by would-be assassin Arthur Bremer. The injuries left him paralyzed.

In the 1970s, according to his biographers, Wallace apologized to his black constituents and to civil rights leaders for his earlier segregationist views. During his last term as governor (1983–1987), he appointed a record number of African Americans to government positions.

George Wallace stands at the entrance to the University of Alabama to prevent admittance of two black students in 1963.

again, the presence of federal troops was required to ensure the black students' safety.

Despite the success of James Meredith and others at the university level, segregation on college campuses persisted in the South for many years. Moreover, many southern states continued to provide far less money to institutions that had been previously reserved for blacks. As late as the mid-1980s, for instance, most of Mississippi's funding went to its five predominantly white universities. As a result, many black universities were unable to improve or repair old, dilapidated classrooms, much less build newer ones. In addition, the lack of funding prevented black colleges from hiring new professors or providing comfortable housing for their students.

On June 26, 1992, in *United States v. Fordice*, the U.S. Supreme Court, in an eight-to-one decision, addressed this situation when it ruled that Mississippi would have to provide more money for the black universities. Justice Byron White wrote, "If the state perpetuates policies and practices traceable to its prior system that continues to have a segregative effect . . . the state has not satisfied its burden of proving that it has dismantled its previous system."[88]

Affirmative Action

Despite federal intervention, African American admissions to previously all-white universities and colleges overall did not significantly increase during the early to mid-1960s. Many black students simply were unwilling to subject themselves to the kind of harassment and intimidation that Meredith had faced. Others were told they were not academically qualified for admission or that they did not qualify for scholarships. Unable to obtain the money to attend primarily white universities, many African Americans applied and were accepted, instead, at black institutions.

The situation for black students did not improve until after the passage of affirmative action legislation in the late 1960s and early 1970s. According to historians Joseph L. White and James H. Cones III, "Affirmative action is the general rubric [name] for a series of programs designed to increase the range of educational, economic, and legal opportunities available to blacks, other minorities, and women."[89]

The affirmative action programs dramatically changed the composition of student bodies on American campuses throughout the country—both North and South. Universities were now required by law to increase their admissions of African American students. Thousands of blacks applied for college and were accepted in large numbers. Schools that had made admission difficult for African Americans in the past were now obligated to offer scholarships to qualified black students as well as consider all applications without regard to race.

Controversy quickly developed as affirmative action programs were implemented across the country. White students, even those who had no objection to integration, became concerned when they saw spaces, which were limited in number, going to less-qualified black applicants. The fact that qualified blacks had long been denied admission in favor of less-qualified whites was not disputed. Nonetheless, many white students protested that they were being penalized for discrimination that others had been guilty of in the past.

Challenges to affirmative action came almost immediately. The man, however, who became identified with these challenges was a thirty-three-year-old former U.S. Marines captain named Allan Bakke. After serving in the armed forces and becoming an aerospace engineer, Bakke applied to the University of California at Davis Medical School. Despite having impressive academic credentials, his application was denied.

Bakke pressed the issue for four years, contending that many of the minority applicants who had been accepted to the medical school had lower test scores than he did. At the time of his lawsuit, the University of California was setting aside sixteen of its one hundred first-year positions for minority students. Bakke charged that this was reverse discrimination.

The *Bakke* Decision

Bakke's lawsuit, *The Regents of the University of California v. Bakke*, was ultimately appealed to the U.S. Supreme Court. On June 28, 1978, the Court ruled five to four in favor of Bakke and ordered his admission to the university. The Court stated that race alone could not be a factor in the admission of minority groups to college. Historian Alphonso Pinkney comments on the majority decision: "The supporters of Bakke . . . felt that the long history of racial oppression in the United States was . . . [over] and that minorities had achieved parity with whites. Some even maintained that affirmative action had actually tipped the scale in favor of minorities."[90]

Thurgood Marshall, who had been appointed to the Supreme Court in 1965, was one of the four justices who disagreed with the majority opinion. He wrote at the time, "In light of the sorry history of discrimination and its devastating impact on the lives of Negroes, bringing the Negro into the mainstream of American life should be a state interest of the highest order. To fail to do so

Allan Bakke smiles after his first day at the University of California at Davis, whose medical school was compelled by the Supreme Court to admit him in 1978.

A Victory for Affirmative Action

Two cases challenging affirmative action at the University of Michigan received very different outcomes from the U.S. Supreme Court. The earlier decision, in 1995, had concluded that the university's actions violated the Equal Protection Clause of the Fourteenth Amendment when admission was denied to white applicant Jennifer Gratz.

Two years later another case from the same university appeared on the Court's docket. Barbara Grutter, a white resident of Michigan, had been denied admission to the law school. She claimed that her race had prevented her acceptance. As before, the case was appealed to the Supreme Court. In this case, however, the Court ruled, in a five-to-four decision, that the university's policies did not violate the Constitution.

Justice Sandra Day O'Connor read the majority opinion: "Because the Law School conducts an individualized review of each applicant, no acceptance or rejection is based on a variable such as race and that this process ensures that all factors that may contribute to diversity are meaningfully considered alongside race." The Court thus concluded that the Michigan program did not practice reverse discrimination.

Quoted in Oyez: U.S. Supreme Court Multimedia, "Grutter v. Bollinger." www.oyez.org/oyez/resource/case/1541.

is to insure that America will forever remain a divided society."[91]

Most African Americans consider the *Bakke* decision a major setback to deseregation. Pinkney summarizes, "Rather than discriminate against non-minorities, the Bakke decision has served to strip minority people of the small gains they have achieved through their long and difficult struggle."[92] Bakke's victory encouraged many other white students to challenge affirmative action. This had an immediate effect on black admissions to universities throughout the country.

To further solidify the Court's decision, California voters in November 1996 went to the polls to vote on Proposition 209, a measure calling for the end of affirmative action in that state.

Passed by a small margin, the proposition forbade the use of race as a basis for admitting students to California colleges. Mark Rosenbaum of the American Civil Liberties Union of Southern California criticizes the vote in favor of this initiative: "For the first time in our nation's history, state and local governments have been stripped of their authority to remedy racial and gender discrimination. . . . California is . . . the only state unwilling to stand up and take strong measures against . . . racial discrimination within its border."[93] Since the passage of Proposition 209, the number of blacks and other minorities on California campuses has significantly decreased. The use of quotas for scholarship purposes was also disallowed.

This legislation in California was but one symptom of what many found a disturbing trend. As the last decade of the twentieth century closed, a move toward the resegregation of America's schools was gaining momentum.

Chapter Six

The Resegregation of America's Schools

Today, more than fifty years after the *Brown* decision, few Americans seriously question anyone's right to an equal opportunity to learn. Instead, the debate is over whether that equality has been achieved, and if not, what the best course might be to achieve it. Despite much progress toward equality, many of today's scholars worry that the gains made immediately after *Brown* have largely been erased. Historian Grace Elizabeth Hale explains, "Today, . . . decades after *Brown*, American public schools stand more segregated by race . . . than at any time in our history."[94]

Resegregation

Dual school systems persist throughout the country. An alarming trend called resegregation, has been taking place in American schools since the mid-1980s. Historians John Hope Franklin and Alfred A. Moss Jr. explain that after the 1970s in the South, "a considerable amount of resegregation occurred as white and black students were racially separated by classes or as black students were excluded from extracurricular activities."[95] While

Concerned about segregation trends in American schools, University of Michigan students demonstrate their support for affirmative action in 1998.

educators accept that some separation will occur as a result of the students choosing to stay with their own racial group, they are more concerned by school officials who assign students to classes according to race. As a result, at the turn of the twenty-first century, the United States is still grappling with the problem of segregation. More than 70 percent of the nation's black students, for instance, still attend predominantly black schools.

What sociologists say is that the majority of white students today have little contact with students of color. As in the past, this is largely due to housing patterns. Whereas metropolitan school districts today are primarily black, suburban schools remain mostly white. What stands out for some observers is where school desegregation seems to have worked best. "Ironically," historian Robinson explains, "the southern states that once most strictly enforced legal separation are today among those where black and white students are most integrated."[96] Instead, New York, where there was no federal intervention and where residential segregation still exists, now holds the distinction for the state that has the most segregated schools in the country.

Most educators and civil rights leaders remain committed to the concept of integrated education. These leaders, however, are meeting with opposition from the broader community, both white and black, as political scientist Jennifer Hochschild explains: "Despite their abstract support for school desegregation, most white members of the American public simply do not want very many black . . . children in the same classroom as their own children. . . . Most black members of the American public either return the compliment or have abandoned the desegregative effort in disgust."[97]

Inequality in Education

After the *Brown* decision was handed down, most Americans assumed that desegregation would address and correct the lack of educational opportunities available to black students. In addition, it was hoped that once African American children were enrolled in decent schools with qualified teachers that their academic achievements would increase. Clearly, *Brown* did result in a dramatic growth in opportunity for black students, but what concerns many is that despite the billions of dollars spent on education, there has been no significant improvement in academic achievement.

Educators point to differences between whites and blacks in their performance on standardized tests. A study done by the Educational Trust concludes that, "by the end of the fourth grade, African American . . . students are already two years behind grade level—by the time they reach the twelfth grade they are four years behind."[98]

Also alarming to some observers is that even in integrated schools, unequal treatment of minority versus white students is noticeable. This inequality extends to the disciplining of students, including the use of suspension, expulsion, and other forms of punishment. Historian Roy L. Brooks elaborates, "African American students, on average, are suspended at a younger age, for a longer time, and more often than whites."[99] In some parts of the country, the rate is from five to ten times higher than for whites. Historians Joseph L. White and James H. Cones III agree: "From the middle of elementary school and continuing into high school, black males lead all other groups of students in suspensions, expulsions, behavioral problems, and referrals to special classes for slow learners."[100] Scholars note that this inequality, especially in inner-city schools, has impacted the drop-out rate for black males and increased it to more than 50 percent.

There are other indications of inequality in today's schools as well. Most blacks, for instance, walk to school or take the bus; white students usually drive or are driven to school. Whereas most blacks eat lunch in the cafeteria, whites often leave campus to eat at fast-food restaurants. The majority of children of both races spend time with friends from their own neighborhoods; there is little racial mixing except in school-sponsored team sports.

In-Class Segregation

Even within desegregated and racially balanced schools, a form of segregation called in-class segregation is occurring with increasing frequency. This particular kind of segregation groups youngsters according to what the staff sees as their "ability to learn." Where such grouping is practiced, individual classrooms often are predominantly black or white.

Magnet Schools

Faced with the knowledge that African American students in both segregated and desegregated school settings were still struggling academically, educators in many areas developed what today are called magnet schools. These schools, based on the premise that not all students learn in the same way or at the same rate, were primarily developed to offer alternative ways for black students to learn. Students could sign up for specific subjects and generally take charge of their own learning and the speed with which they learned. Without the academic competition and in-class segregation found at many public schools, it was hoped that African American students could benefit from a less stressful, less regimented, and more open school setting. The term *magnet schools* came from an observation in Houston, Texas, where a local school worked like a magnet in attracting students.

When created in the late 1960s, magnet schools emphasized the basic subjects of reading, writing, and mathematics, but they also offered courses in African American history and information about the civil rights movement. Some of the earlier schools, called street academies, led to more permanent structures such as Harlem Prep in New York City. Initially funded by private foundations, the school eventually became part of the public school system of New York. By 1980 most major cities had magnet school systems of one type or another.

Students chant an inspirational motto at a successful magnet school in Kansas City, Missouri, in 2006.

Tracking, the grouping of students by perceived potential to perform in the classroom, is common in America's schools. This often results in segregation by race. Few blacks, for instance, are ever labeled as *gifted*. "About half of all black students are in low achievement reading groups, compared to one-fifth for whites," historian Brooks explains. "Such racial disparity . . . isolates students, associates skin color with skill, and leads parents, teachers, and students alike to expect little . . . from blacks."[101] The impact of tracking is most evident in the race of those students selected to take honors and college-preparatory courses. In Louisville, Kentucky, for instance, although the schools are 30 percent black, the percentage of African Americans in honors classes is only 10 percent; in Cleveland, Ohio, the numbers are 50 percent and 10 percent. Experts suggest that bias is the reason. Most African American students, they say, are arbitrarily denied placement in honors groups primarily because of low expectations among white teachers and counselors.

This kind of in-class discrimination begins as early as kindergarten. An African American mother from Raleigh, North Carolina, spoke with host Neal Conan on National Public Radio about her child, who is in the public school system there: "I've found . . . that while the schools are integrated, the children within the schools aren't being treated equally." She talked of sending her child to kindergarten and on the first day of school, the teacher

Film director Spike Lee speaks on cultural diversity at the University of Mississippi in February 2006 during Black History month.

told him, "It's okay if you get C's. C's are good grades. Be happy with them."[102] The mother, believing her son was not getting the kind of nurturing and encouragement that his white classmates were receiving, later removed him from that school district.

Reporter Joe Smith believes that many teachers are still not ready to accept that African Americans are just as capable of learning as white students. He reports from Ohio, "Cleveland's minority students still suffer from teachers who think they can't learn. . . . This prejudicial thinking becomes a self-fulfilling prophecy that manifests itself in the poor grades of African American students."[103] Historian Robinson, a former Los Angeles high school student, reinforces this idea: "I can remember a white high school counselor telling me . . . that I should look into being a cook rather than the lawyer I said I wanted to be."[104]

Trends in College Education

Students continue to face racial inequality as they go on to college. Despite an increase in African American enrollment at the university level, prejudice and discrimination also still exist on college campuses throughout the country. Today at the University of Mississippi, for instance, segregation is still apparent on campus and in extracurricular life. Mark Carve, a former student at Ole Miss, reported in 2002, "Well after James Meredith enrolled at Ole Miss, blacks remained on the fringes of campus life. . . . The school tries to paint a certain picture of what it's all about. But when you get here and live here, especially as a minority, you get to see how it's still the same. It's still racist."[105] This is most clearly evident in the racial composition of many clubs, fraternities, and alumni functions.

This discrimination also extends to the hiring and promotion of African American faculty. Historian Brooks elaborates on how this plays out in law schools, for example:

> Some white law professors are predisposed to assess the performance of African American law professors in a negative or hypercritical fashion, are intolerant of even small mistakes committed by these scholars, and tend to deny African Americans the deference or presumption of competence normally accorded to white male law professors.[106]

As a result, some say, the percentage of minority teachers at law schools is low compared to those of white professors, less than 5 percent in many areas.

Another trend that alarms educators is the increasing number of African American college students who drop out before completing their degrees. In 1980, for instance, whites were twice as likely to graduate as blacks; the difference has since intensified. Barely one in seven African Americans who starts college finishes it. Historian Robinson, who taught at Rutgers University, explains that part of the problem may be students' perceptions of their own ability. "Too many of my black students believed they were less intelligent than their white counterparts and consequently did not put forth the kind of effort that was needed."[107]

Most educators today believe that the shortage of college-educated African Americans has potentially long-term repercussions on American society as a whole. It limits the supply of black role models, community leaders, and teachers. To correct this imbalance, many African American leaders are urging the recruitment of young blacks to be teachers. They advocate the creation of scholarships and other incentives for blacks who want to teach. As Brooks summarizes, "Increasing the ranks of college-educated African Americans must become a top priority of the nation."[108]

Working Toward Equality

Today's educators, black and white, are working to find innovative ways to address resegregation and the inequality that still exists in America's public schools. Some have put forward the idea that separate, even segregated, schools with equal funding may be a better option than desegregation. A 1998 poll, in fact, revealed that both black and white parents believed that raising student achievement and academic standards were more important than integration.

One way to accomplish true equality, black educators believe, is to leave predominantly African American schools, from the elementary to the university level, in the hands of black teachers and administrators. The primary problem, however, with this concept is funding. In most areas of the country, white politicians and white educators still control most of the resources that are needed to equalize educational opportunities for blacks and whites.

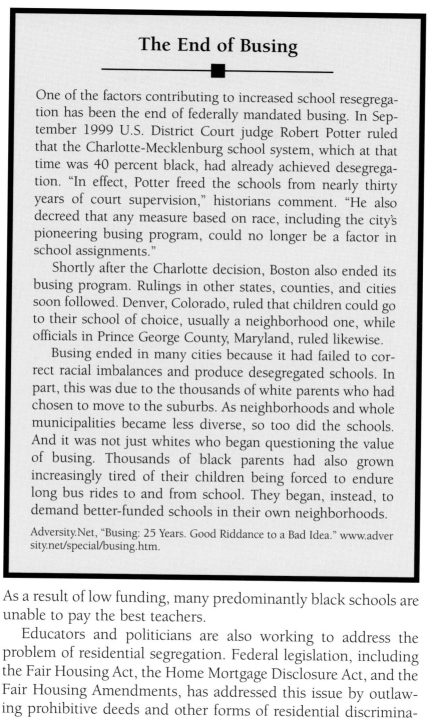

The End of Busing

One of the factors contributing to increased school resegregation has been the end of federally mandated busing. In September 1999 U.S. District Court judge Robert Potter ruled that the Charlotte-Mecklenburg school system, which at that time was 40 percent black, had already achieved desegregation. "In effect, Potter freed the schools from nearly thirty years of court supervision," historians comment. "He also decreed that any measure based on race, including the city's pioneering busing program, could no longer be a factor in school assignments."

Shortly after the Charlotte decision, Boston also ended its busing program. Rulings in other states, counties, and cities soon followed. Denver, Colorado, ruled that children could go to their school of choice, usually a neighborhood one, while officials in Prince George County, Maryland, ruled likewise.

Busing ended in many cities because it had failed to correct racial imbalances and produce desegregated schools. In part, this was due to the thousands of white parents who had chosen to move to the suburbs. As neighborhoods and whole municipalities became less diverse, so too did the schools. And it was not just whites who began questioning the value of busing. Thousands of black parents had also grown increasingly tired of their children being forced to endure long bus rides to and from school. They began, instead, to demand better-funded schools in their own neighborhoods.

Adversity.Net, "Busing: 25 Years. Good Riddance to a Bad Idea." www.adver sity.net/special/busing.htm.

As a result of low funding, many predominantly black schools are unable to pay the best teachers.

Educators and politicians are also working to address the problem of residential segregation. Federal legislation, including the Fair Housing Act, the Home Mortgage Disclosure Act, and the Fair Housing Amendments, has addressed this issue by outlawing prohibitive deeds and other forms of residential discrimination. In increasing numbers, African Americans are moving to previously all-white suburbs and taking advantage of the quality school systems located there.

Indianapolis, Indiana, is one of the cities that is using this kind of innovative plan to correct educational inequality. Officials from the Indianapolis Housing Authority, the state, and the Justice Department are working together to assist low-income and minority families in finding affordable housing in the suburbs. Although these efforts may help some families, they do not address the many problems faced by inner-city school districts, particularly the lack of funding.

Many schools are trying to stimulate greater achievement by black children. This effort began with Operation Head Start, a program designed to improve the preparation of preschoolers for public school. Head Start is a federally funded child development program that provides services to young children from low-income families, both black and white. According to the Alabama Head Start Program, "The Head Start concept of early childhood education is a comprehensive program designed to meet the emotional, social, health, nutritional, and psychological needs of children of low income families. . . . Head Start provides these children with the opportunity to enter public school with a 'head start' willing and able to learn."[109] While not specifically designed for African American children, Head Start programs across the country have been helpful in improving the chances for black children to succeed in school.

Desegregation Can Work

Despite what some policy makers see as the alarming trend toward resegregation, many cities have found innovative ways to make desegregation work. In Dayton, Ohio, for instance, the primary factor that led to the success of its desegregation program was the fact that the school committee provided the community with numerous ways to become personally involved in implementing the plan. Advisory boards, for example, were formed that included business and religious leaders, social agencies, the police department, parents, and even a few of the students themselves. These interracial boards, able to address the needs of both races, managed to develop workable plans for integrating the city's school district. These plans included busing, increasing funding to

Afrocentric Schools

The belief that African American children do not need desegregated classes in order to learn has been shared by many black leaders. As far back as the early 1950s, many blacks were critical of the *Brown* decision for this reason. Distinguished African American novelist Zora Neale Hurston was among the critics. According to historians Stephen and Abigail Thernstrom in their book *America in Black and White*, "Hurston rejected as false what she took to be the premise underlying Brown—that black children required the presence of white people in order to learn—and saw the decision as insulting rather than honoring her race." Many blacks continue to feel that it is patronizing to think that minority students need to attend desegregated schools in order to learn and benefit from an education.

As a result of pressure from African American academicians and activists, many schools adopted an Afrocentric curriculum. "This kind of curriculum highlights African and African American history and culture," historians Joseph L. White and James H. Cones III write in their book *Black Man Emerging*. "Children are taught to be proud of the heroic liberation struggle Black people in America have waged against overwhelming odds." These programs have helped blacks develop a stronger sense of ethnic pride and a stronger sense of their own identity and culture that has enabled them to work for social change in areas such as race relations, politics, and education. Currently there are more than four hundred such schools in this country.

Students at an Afrocentric school in Chicago finish their classes for the day.

Stephen and Abigail Thernstrom, *America in Black and White: One Nation, Indivisible: Race in Modern America.* New York: Simon and Schuster, 1997, p. 318.

Joseph L. White and James H. Cones III, *Black Man Emerging: Facing the Past and Seizing the Future in America.* New York: W.H. Freeman, 1999, p. 259.

inner-city schools, and teacher exchanges between suburban and inner-city schools. This cooperation enabled the committee to work together to achieve successful desegregation in the city.

Observers say that cooperation between African American and white community members is essential to successful desegregation. Cross-racial groups have worked cooperatively to produce racially balanced schools in many school districts. By discussing potential problems, the groups have, in many cases, reduced the violence that accompanied so many integration attempts in the past. This cooperation extends to the students themselves. Students of both races are encouraged to meet in small groups to address any problems that occur within their schools. This cooperation and interaction between the races has helped to significantly reduce racial tension and antagonism.

Political scientist Hochschild believes that there are three elements that must be present to achieve such success: One is leadership by school officials who are able to actively promote the value of integration. There should also be incentives to encourage parents to participate in the decision-making process. Lastly there has to be active cooperation by officials at all levels of government. Hochschild summarizes that, "when coupled with deep systemic reform of educational governance and content, [desegregation] is our only available option for ending the racial isolation and . . . racial antagonism that separates cities and suburbs."[110]

What Does the Future Hold?

Despite numerous success stories and many new and innovative ways to achieve racial equality in education, numerous challenges remain. Educators and social scientists believe that the most critical one is the continued presence of racist thinking and action in the United States. "I think that one thing that we need to remember when we're talking about racial integration or desegregation in schools," states Susan Eaton of the Civil Rights Project at Harvard University, "is that schools are part of a larger society. And we live in an incredibly race-conscious, racist society still. . . . Whites control economics and politics to a very large extent, and because of that, separate is still highly unequal."[111]

Notes

Introduction:
Centuries of Discrimination

1. Joseph L. White and James H. Cones III, *Black Man Emerging: Facing the Past and Seizing the Future in America*. New York: W. H. Freeman, 1999, p. 259.
2. Leon F. Litwack, *Trouble in Mind: Black Southerners in the Age of Jim Crow*. New York: Alfred A. Knopf, 1998, p. 53.
3. Quoted in Douglas O. Linder, "Before *Brown:* Charles H. Houston and the *Gaines* Case," 2000. www.law.umkc.edu/faculty/projects/ftrials/trialheroes/charleshoustonessayF.html.
4. Quoted in Roy L. Brooks, *Rethinking the American Race Problem*. Berkeley and Los Angeles: University of California Press, 1990, p. 76.

Chapter One: Jim Crow:
Separate but Unequal

5. Quoted in Sanford Wexler, *The Civil Rights Movement*. New York: Facts On File, 1993, p. 22.
6. Doug Linder, "*Plessy v. Ferguson*," 2006. www.law.umkc.edu/faculty/projects/ftrials/conlaw/plessy.html.
7. Litwack, *Trouble in Mind*, p. 95.
8. Benjamin E. Mays, "The Moral Aspects of Segregation" speech, Twenty-first Annual Meeting of the Southern Historical Society, November 10, 1955.
9. Litwack, *Trouble in Mind*, p. 107.
10. Ray Sprigle, "A Visit to a Jim Crow School," *Pittsburgh Post-Gazette*, 1998. www.post-gazette.com/sprigle/199808spriglechap13.asp.
11. David R. Goldfield, *Black, White, and Southern: Race Relations and Southern Culture, 1940 to the Present*. Baton Rouge: Louisiana State University Press, 1990, p. 57.
12. Litwack, *Trouble in Mind*, p. 106.
13. Sprigle, "A Visit to a Jim Crow School."
14. Quoted in Wexler, *The Civil Rights Movement*, p. 9.
15. Arlington National Cemetery Website, "Thurgood Marshall, Associate Justice, United States Supreme Court," November 3, 2005. www.arlingtoncemetery.net/tmarsh.htm.
16. Goldfield, *Black, White, and Southern*, p. 59.
17. Quoted in Goldfield, *Black, White, and Southern*, p. 59.

Chapter Two:
A Landmark Decision

18. Stephen and Abigail Thernstrom, *America in Black and White: One Nation, Indivisible: Race in Modern*

America. New York: Simon and Schuster, 1997, p. 99.

19. Quoted in Wexler, *The Civil Rights Movement*, p. 42.

20. Wexler, *The Civil Rights Movement*, p. 34.

21. Quoted in Carl T. Rowan, *Dream Makers, Dream Breakers: The World of Justice Thurgood Marshall.* Boston: Little, Brown, 1993, p. 184.

22. Quoted in Wexler, *The Civil Rights Movement*, p. 45.

23. Quoted in Wexler, *The Civil Rights Movement*, p. 36.

24. Robert Weisbrot, *Freedom Bound: A History of America's Civil Rights Movement.* New York: W.W. Norton, 1990, p. 11.

25. Quoted in Wexler, *The Civil Rights Movement*, p. 34.

26. *Brown v. Board of Education*, 347 U.S. 483 (1954).

27. Thernstrom, *America in Black and White*, p. 97.

28. David Halberstam, *The Fifties.* New York: Fawcett Columbine, 1993, p. 423.

29. Quoted in Wexler, *The Civil Rights Movement*, p. 48.

30. Weisbrot, *Freedom Bound*, p. 11

31. Quoted in Wexler, *The Civil Rights Movement*, p. 49.

32. Quoted in U.S. Congress, "Southern Manifesto: Declaration of Constitutional Principles," 84th Cong., 2nd sess., *Congressional Record*, March 12, 1956.

33. Quoted in Rowan, *Dream Makers, Dream Breakers*, p. 277.

34. Brian Lamb, *Booknotes: Stories from American History.* New York: Penguin, 2002, p. 330.

Chapter Three: The South's Fight Against Desegregation

35. Harry S. Ashmore, *Civil Rights and Wrongs: A Memoir of Race and Politics: 1944–1994.* New York: Pantheon, 1994, p, 154.

36. John Patterson, Alabama gubernatorial inauguration speech, January 20, 1959.

37. Goldfield, *Black, White, and Southern*, p. 80

38. Mary C. Doyle, "From Desegregation to Resegregation: Public Schools in Norfolk, VA, 1954–2002," *Journal of African American History*, 2005. www.highbeam.com/library.

39. Goldfield, *Black, White, and Southern*, p. 116.

40. Goldfield, *Black, White, and Southern*, p. 82.

41. Thernstrom, *America in Black and White*, p. 106.

42. Quoted in Ashmore, *Civil Rights and Wrongs*, p. 115.

43. *Journal of Southern History*, "A Continuity of Conservatism: The Limitations of *Brown v. Board of Education*," 2004. www.highbeam.com/library.

44. Quoted in Goldfield, *Black, White, and Southern*, p. 109.

45. Quoted in Doyle, "From Desegregation to Resegregation."

46. Quoted in Wexler, *The Civil Rights Movement*, p. 91.

47. Lamb, *Booknotes*, p. 331.
48. Halberstam, *The Fifties*, p. 685.
49. Quoted in Stephen E. Ambrose, *Eisenhower: Soldier and President.* York: Touchstone, 1990, p. 447.
50. Quoted in Wexler, *The Civil Rights Movement*, p. 101.
51. Halberstam, *The Fifties*, p. 687.
52. Halberstam, *The Fifties*, p. 688.
53. Melba Pattillo Beals, *Warriors Don't Cry.* New York: Washington Square, 1994, p. 1.
54. Quoted in Wexler, *The Civil Rights Movement*, p. 104.
55. Arkansas Online, "Little Rock's Lost Class of 1959," September 27, 1998. www.ardemgaz.com/prev/central/acclass27.html.
56. Quoted in Arkansas Online, "Little Rock's Lost Class of 1959."
57. Quoted in Arkansas Online, "Little Rock's Lost Class of 1959."
58. Quoted in Goldfield, *Black, White, and Southern*, p. 111.
59. John Hope Franklin and Alfred A. Moss Jr., *From Slavery to Freedom: A History of African Americans.* New York: Alfred A. Knopf, 2004, p. 547.
60. Quoted in Jane Fullerton, "Little Rock Nine Recognized for Heroism," Arkansas Online, November 10, 1999. www.ardemgaz.com/prev/central/abxnine10.html.

Chapter Four:
The North: De Facto Segregation

61. Thernstrom, *America in Black and White*, p. 325.
62. Touro Law Center, "*Swann v. Charlotte-Mecklenburg Board of Education.*" www.tourolaw.edu/patch/Swann.
63. Weisbrot, *Freedom Bound*, p. 289.
64. Thernstrom, *America in Black and White*, p. 327.
65. Thernstrom, *America in Black and White*, p. 335.
66. Lisa Cozzens, "School Integration (1955–1975)." *African American History*, May 25, 1998. http://fledge.watson.org/~lisa/blackhistory/citing.html.
67. Lisa Cozzens, "School Integration in Boston." www.4littlegirls.com/boston.htm.
68. Grace Elizabeth Hale, *Making Whiteness: The Culture of Segregation in the South.* New York Random House, 1998, p. 289.
69. Quoted in Cozzens, "School Integration in Boston."
70. Quoted in Cozzens, "School Integration in Boston."
71. Quoted in Neal Conan, "Analysis: School Desegregation and Busing," *Talk of the Nation*, National Public Radio, April 22, 2002.
72. Quoted in Conan, "Analysis: School Desegregation and Busing."
73. Quoted in Conan, "Analysis: School Desegregation and Busing."
74. Quoted in Alphonso Pinkney, *The Myth of Black Progress.* London: Cambridge University Press, 1984, p. 139.
75. Rowan, *Dream Makers, Dream Breakers*, p. 371.
76. Quoted in Thernstrom, *America in Black and White*, p. 330.

Chapter Five: Breaking the Color Barrier on College Campuses

77. Litwack, *Trouble in Mind*, p. 83.
78. Thernstrom, *America in Black and White*, p. 115.
79. Quoted in Thernstrom, *America in Black and White*, p. 97.
80. Quoted in Candace D. Fisk, "James Meredith at Ole Miss: Victory over Discrimination," *National Council for the Social Studies*, 2004. www.highbeam.com/library.
81. Robert Dallek, *An Unfinished Life: John F. Kennedy*. Boston: Little, Brown, 2003, p. 514.
82. Quoted in Fisk, "James Meredith at Ole Miss." www.highbeam.com/library.
83. Quoted in Wexler, *The Civil Rights Movement*, p. 144.
84. Quoted in Wexler, *The Civil Rights Movement*, p. 155.
85. Quoted in William Doyle, *An American Insurrection: The Battle of Oxford, Mississippi, 1962*. New York: Doubleday, 2001, p. 263.
86. Quoted in Wexler, *The Civil Rights Movement*, p. 156.
87. Quoted in Goldfield, *Black, White, and Southern*, p. 115.
88. Quoted in Rowan, *Dream Makers, Dream Breakers*, p. 336.
89. White and Cones, *Black Man Emerging*, p. 83.
90. Pinkney, *The Myth of Black Progress*, p. 152.
91. Quoted in Arlington National Cemetery Web site, "Thurgood Marshall: Associate Justice, United States Supreme Court," November 3, 2005. www.arlingtoncemetery.net/tmarsh.htm.
92. Pinkney, *The Myth of Black Progress*, pp. 154–55.
93. Quoted in *AAD Project*, "Proposition 209," November 28, 2001. http://aad.english.ucsb.edu/pages/PROP-209.html.

Chapter Six: The Resegregation of America's Schools

94. Hale, *Making Whiteness*, p. 289.
95. Franklin and Moss, *From Slavery to Freedom*, p. 548.
96. James L. Robinson, *Racism or Attitude? The Ongoing Struggle for Black Liberation and Self-Esteem*. New York: Insight, 1995, p. 171.
97. Jennifer Hochschild, "Is School Desegregation Still a Viable Option?" *Political Science and Politics*, 1997. www.highbeam.com/library.
98. Quoted in Victor Goode, "The Future of *Brown*," *Colorlines*, June 6, 2004.
99. Brooks, *Rethinking the American Race Problem*, p. 77.
100. White and Cones, *Black Man Emerging*, p. 259.
101. Brooks, *Rethinking the American Race Problem*, p. 77.
102. Quoted in Neal Conan, "Analysis: History of Desegregation in America and a New Trend Toward Resegregation in Public Schools," *Talk of the Nation*, National Public Radio, September 25, 2002.
103. Quoted in Susan Stamberg, "Cleve-

land School Desegregation Ruling," *Weekend Saturday*, National Public Radio, December 27, 1997.

104. Robinson, *Racism or Attitude?* p. 60.

105. Quoted in Robert Siegel and Jacki Lyden, "Profile: University of Mississippi Forty Years After the Enrollment of James Meredith," *All Things Considered*, National Public Radio, September 30, 2002.

106. Brooks, *Rethinking the American Race Problem*, p. 48.

107. Robinson, *Racism or Attitude?* pp. 22–23.

108. Brooks, *Rethinking the American Race Problem*, p. 82.

109. Southeast Alabama Regional Planning and Development Commission, "Headstart Program." www.sanman.net/searpdc/headstart/headastart.htm.

110. Hochschild, "Is School Desegregation Still a Viable Option?"

111. Quoted in Conan, "Analysis: School Desegregation and Busing."

For More Information

Books

Linda Jacobs Altman, *The American Civil Rights Movement: The African-American Struggle for Equality.* Berkeley Heights, NJ: Enslow, 2004. This book covers slavery through the present day, with emphasis on the struggle of blacks for equal rights.

Melba Pattillo Beals, *Warriors Don't Cry.* New York: Washington Square, 1994. A memoir written by one of the Little Rock Nine. She began the first draft of the book when she was eighteen.

Reggie Finlayson, *We Shall Overcome: The History of the American Civil Rights Movement.* Minneapolis: Lerner, 2003. This book covers the civil rights events from 1955 to 1963.

Jim Haskins, *Separate but Not Equal: The Dream and the Struggle.* New York: Scholastic, 1998. This is an outstanding reference that focuses solely on black education and the desegregation of America's schools.

Milton Meltzer, *There Comes a Time: The Struggle for Civil Rights.* New York: Random House, 2001. A book about the civil rights movement.

Walter Dean Myers, *Now Is Your Time! The African-American Struggle for Freedom.* New York: HarperCollins, 1991. A book about the many people whose lives made a difference in the struggle for equality.

Amy Polakow, *Daisy Bates: Civil Rights Crusader.* North Haven, CT: Linnet, 2003. This is an excellent biography of Daisy Bates, the moving force behind the Little Rock, Arkansas, desegregation movement.

Fred Powledge, *We Shall Overcome: Heroes of the Civil Rights Movement.* New York: Charles Scribner's Sons, 1993. A book about the hundreds of people, black and white, who worked for equality.

Elizabeth Sirimarco, *The Civil Rights Movement.* New York: Benchmark, 2005. The author examines many aspects of the civil rights movement.

Mildred Pitts Walter, *Mississippi Challenge.* New York: Bradbury, 1992. The author grew up in Mississippi and describes the effects of segregation on her life.

Internet Sources

Arkansas Online, "The Crisis Mr. Faubus Made," September 4, 1957. www.ar demgaz.com/prev/central/wgaz04.html.

———, "Governor Faubus Got His Answer," September 15, 1957. www. ardemgaz.com/prev/central/wgaz15.ht ml.

———, "Little Rock's Lost Class of 1959," September 27, 1998. www.ar demgaz.com/prev/acclass27.html.

————, "Time Line: The Stage Is Set," 1997. www.ardemgaz.com/prev/central/CHSmain.html.

————, "What Now in Our School Trouble?" September 5, 1957. www.ardemgaz.com/prev/central/wdem05.html.

Center for History and New Media, "Thurgood Marshall, Supreme Court Justice." www.chnm.gmu.edu/courses/122/hill/marshall.htm.

Lisa Cozzens, "School Integration in Boston." www.4littlegirls.com/boston.htm.

Jane Fullerton, "Little Rock Nine Recognized for Heroism," November 10, 1999. www.ardemgaz.com/prev/central/abxnine10.html.

Heroism Project, "Melba Pattillo Beals: Breaking the Color Barrier." www.heroism.org/class/1950/heroes/beals.htm.

Jack Schnedler, "What Happened After Central High Crisis?" 1997. www.ardemgaz.com/prev/central/wcentral04.html.

Tavis Smiley, "Analysis: *Brown v. Board of Education* 50 Years Later," National Public Radio *Talk of the Nation*, May 17, 2004. www.highbeam.com/library.

Ray Sprigle, "A Visit to a Jim Crow School," *Pittsburgh Post-Gazette*. www.post-gazette.com/sprigle.

U.S. Marshals Service, "The U.S. Marshals and the Integration of the University of Mississippi: 40 Years Ago and the Present." www.usdoj.gov/marshals/history/miss/04.htm.

Index

abolitionists, 7
affirmative action, 31, 76-80
Africa, 21
African Americans
academic achievement, 83-86, 88, 90
  busing
    effects of, 61, 62-63
    opposition to, 89
  economic reprisals against, 40
  education inequalities, 84-89
  importance to Southern economy of uneducated, 14
  opinion of *Bakke* decision, 79
  opposition to Brown, 91
  pre-Civil War population, 9
  segregated education effects, 24, 26, 28, 29-30, 33-34
  stereotypes of, 15-16
Afrocentric schools, 91
Alabama, 40
Alabama, University of, 66-68, 74, 76
Almond, J. Lindsay, 49
Ambrose, Stephen E., 35
America in Black and White (Thernstrom and Thernstrom), 91
American Dilemma: The Negro Problem in Modern Democracy, The (Myrdal), 21
American Insurrection, An (Doyle), 47
American Missionary Society, 11
Arkansas, 41-49, 51
Arkansas Gazette (newspaper), 49
Arkansas State Press (newspaper), 42
Ashmore, Harry S., 35, 38, 48

Bakke, Allan, 77-79
Barnett, Ross, 70
Bates, Daisy, 42, 45
Bates, Lucius Christopher "L.C.", 42
Belton v. Gephart, 26
Black, White, and Southern (Goldfield), 48
Black Man Emerging (White and Cones), 91
Black Monday, 34
blacks. *See* African Americans
Boston, Massachusetts
  busing, 59-63, 89
  pre-Civil War, 9
  white flight from public schools, 58
boycotts
  economic, 50, 54
  of schools by African Americans, 25
Bremer, Arthur, 75

Briggs, Henry, 24
Brooks, Roy L., 84, 85-86, 87, 88
Brown, Henry Billings, 11
Brown, Leola, 27
Brown, Linda, 27
Brown, Oliver, 27
Brown, Rebecca, 24
Brown II, 37
Brown v. Board of Education of Topeka, Kansas
  African-American opposition, 91
  background, 23-28
  decision, 32-34
  implementation of, 35, 37-39, 40-49, 50-51
  strategy, 29-30, 31
Bulah v. Gephart, 26
Burger, Warren, 56-57
busing
  across district lines, 64
  court ordered, 55, 57, 58
  ending, 89
  response to, 59-63

California, University of, 77-79
California Proposition 209, 79-80
Canterbury, Connecticut, 8-9
Carve, Mark, 87
Central High School. *See* Little Rock, Arkansas
Charlotte, North Carolina, 55-57, 89
Civil Rights Act (1964), 51, 57
Civil Rights and Wrongs (Ashmore), 35, 48
civil rights movement, 17, 71
Clarendon County, South Carolina, 23-25
Clark, Kenneth, 30
Clark, Septima, 17
Clemson University, 74
Cleveland, Ohio, 86, 87
Clinton, Bill, 51
colleges and universities
  affirmative action and, 77-79
  African-American, 65, 76
  resegregation, 87-88
  in South, 18-20, 66-70, 72-74, 76
colonial era, 6-8
Colorado, 58, 89
Cones, James H., III, 6, 76, 84, 91
Crandall, Prudence, 8-9

Dalleck, Robert, 70
Davies, Ronal, 43
Davis Medical School (University of California), 77-79

Dayton, Ohio, 90, 92
Declaration of Constitutional Principles, 34-36
de facto segregation, 52-57, 58, 64, 83
DeLaine, Joseph Albert, 24
Delaware, 26
Denver, Colorado, 58, 89
Detroit, Michigan, 64
Douglas, William O., 35
Doyle, Mary C., 39
Doyle, William, 47

Eaton, Susan, 92
Eckford, Elizabeth, 47
education
    Afrocentric schools, 91
    busing
        across district lines, 64
        court ordered, 55, 57, 58
        ending, 89
        response to, 61-63
    definitions of racial imbalance in schools, 57
    desegregated
        elements of successful, 90, 92
        inequalities in, 84-89
    freedom-of-choice plans, 48
    funding, 39, 51, 88-89
    importance of, 6, 10, 32-33
    magnet schools, 85
    quotas, 55
    resegregation
        California Proposition 209, 79-80
        causes, 81, 83
        results, 83-88, 89
    segregated
        effects, 29-30, 33-34
        extent, 22
        inequality of, 14-16, 24
        during Jim Crow era, 16
        pre-Civil War, 6-9
        during Reconstruction, 10-11
Educational Trust, 84
Eisenhower, Dwight D.
    implementation of Brown, 35, 44-45
    Warren and, 32
Eisenhower: Soldier and President (Ambrose), 35
Elliott, Richard, 72
Ellison, Phyliss, 61
equal protection in Constitution, 11, 29, 34, 79

Faubus, Orville, 43, 46, 49
Fine, Benjamin, 47
Fourteenth Amendment, 11, 29, 34, 79
Franklin, John Hope, 51, 81
Freedman's Bureau schools, 10-11
freedom-of-choice plans, 48

Garrett, Henry, 26
Garrity, W. Arthur, 60
Georgia, University of, 68
gifted programs, 85

girls' boarding schools, 8-9
Goldfield, David R.
    on Green decision, 48
    on inequality of education of African Americans, 16
    on March Against Fear, 71
    on pace of desegregation in South, 39
    on Southern laws to subvert Brown, 39
    on University of Oklahoma response to district court McLaurin decision, 20
    on white citizens' councils, 40
Gore, Albert, Sr., 36
graduate schools
    affirmative action and, 77-80
    early desegregation cases, 18-20, 66-68
    NAACP strategy, 18
    resegregation, 87-88
Gratz, Jennifer, 79
Gray, Garland, 39
Greenberg, Jack, 26
Green v. New Kent County School Board, 48
Grutter, Barbara, 79

Halberstam, David, 34, 44-46
Hale, Grace Elizabeth, 60, 81
Harlem Prep, 85
Head Start, 90
Highlander Folk School, 17
Hill, Oliver, 25-26
Hochschild, Jennifer, 83, 92
Holmes, Hamilton, 68
Hood, James, 74, 76
Horton, Myles, 17
housing patterns
    de facto segregation, 52-55, 64, 83
    federal legislation, 89-90
    white flight, 58
Houston, Charles Hamilton, 18-19, 31
Houston, Texas, 85
Hunter, Charlayne, 68
Hurston, Zora Neale, 91
Hutchinson, Tim, 51

illiteracy, 7
in-class segregation, 84
Indiana, 90
Indianapolis, Indiana, 90
integration vs. desegregation, 57-58

Jackson, Ellen, 61
Jim Crow era, 12-16
Johns, Barbara Rose, 25
Johnson, Lyndon Baines, 31, 36

Katzenbach, Nicholas, 74
Kefauver, Estes, 36
Kennedy, John Fitzgerald, 70, 72, 74
Kentucky, 86
Keyes v. School District Number 1, 58
King, Martin Luther, Jr., 71
Ku Klux Klan, 71

Lamb, Brian, 36, 44
Legal Defense and Education Fund, 18
  graduate school cases, 18-20
  public school cases
    Clarendon County, South Carolina, 24-25
    Delaware, 26
    Prince Edward County, Virginia, 25-26
    Topeka, Kansas, 27-30, 32-34
Legal Redress Committee. See Legal Defense and
  Education Fund
Lexington, Massachusetts, 61
Little Rock, Arkansas, 41-49, 51
Little Rock Nine, 51
Litwack, Leon P., 7, 15, 65
Louisiana, 39, 50
Louisville, Kentucky, 86
Lucy, Autherine, 66-68

magnet schools, 85
Malone, Vivian, 74, 76
March Against Fear, 71
Marshall, Texas, 46
Marshall, Thurgood, 21, 31
  Bakke dissent, 78-79
  graduate school cases, 18-20
  Meredith and, 70
  public school cases, 24-25
  see also Brown v. Board of Education of Topeka,
    Kansas
Maryland, 63, 89
Massachusetts, 58, 61-63, 89
Mays, Benjamin E., 14
McDowell, Claude, 73-74
McLaurin, George, 19-20
McLaurin v. Oklahoma State Regents, 19-20
McMillan, James B., 55
Mecklenburg County, North Carolina, 55-57, 89
media, 45-46, 47, 69, 72
Meredith, James, 68-73
Merida, Kevin, 63
Michigan, 62, 64
Michigan, University of, 79
Milliken, William, 64
Milliken v. Bradley, 64
Milwaukee, Wisconsin, 54
Mississippi, 39, 40
Mississippi, University of, 69-70, 72-74, 87
Mississippi Association of Teachers in Colored
  Schools, 16
Moss, Alfred A., Jr., 51, 81
Myrdal, Gunnar, 21

National Action Group, 62
National Association for the Advancement of Col-
  ored People (NAACP), 18, 54
  see also Legal Defense and Education Fund
Negroes. See African Americans
New Orleans, Louisiana, 50
New York, 83
New York City, 85

Nixon, Richard, 63
North Carolina, 55-57, 89
Northern states
  colleges and universities, 65-66
  current status of segregated education, 83
  de facto segregation, 52-55
  pre-Civil War education of African Americans,
    8-9
  public opinion about segregated schools, 23
  see also specific states

O'Connor, Sandra Day, 79
Ohio, 86, 87, 90, 92
Oklahoma, University of, 19-20
Ole Miss. See Mississippi, University of
Operation Head Start, 90

Patterson, John, 38-39
Pattillo, Melba, 46-47
people of color. See African Americans
Perez, Leander, 50
Phipps, Mamie, 30
Pinkey, Alphonso, 77-78, 79
Plessy, Homer, 11
Plessy v. Ferguson, 11-13, 14-15, 19
Pollock, Earl, 32
Pontiac, Michigan, 62
Potter, Robert, 89
Prince Edward County, Virginia, 25-26
Prince George County, Maryland, 63, 89
private schools, 39, 50
professional schools. See graduate schools
public opinion
  about academic achievement, 88
  about discrimination, 21
  about segregated schools, 23
public schools
  desegregation in
    North and West, 26, 54, 58-63
    South, 41-51, 55-57
  inequalities in integrated, 84-87, 89
  white flight from, 58

Quakers, 7

racial superiority theories, 13-14
Reconstruction, 10-11
Redding, Louis, 26
Regents of the University of California v. Bakke, The,
  77-79
religious groups, 7, 11
resegregation
  California Proposition 209, 79-80
  causes, 81, 83, 89
  colleges and universities, 87-88
  results, 83-87, 89
Rhodes, Ritgerod, 49
Robert R. Moton High School, 25-26
Roberts, Benjamin F., 9
Robinson, Spottswood, 25-26, 83, 87, 88

Rosenbaum, Mark, 80
Rothwell, Angus, 54
Rowan, Carl T., 64
Roxbury, Massachusetts, 59-61

segregation
    de facto, 52-57
    in-class, 84
    purpose of, 14
Seitz, Collins, 26
separate but equal doctrine, 12-13, 14-15, 19, 29, 34
Sitton, Claude, 72
slave codes, 7
Smith, Don, 49
Smith, Gene, 44
Smith, Joe, 87
Smith, M. Brewster, 26
South Boston, Massachusetts, 59-61
South Carolina, 22, 23-25, 39, 74
Southern Manifesto, 34-36
Southern states
    colleges and universities, 18-20, 66-70, 72-74, 76
    education
        current status, 83
        during Jim Crow era, 16
        pre-Civil War, 6-7
        public opinion about, 23
        during Reconstruction, 10-11
    importance of uneducated African Americans to economy, 14
    reaction to Brown, 34-37, 38-41
    see also specific states
Soviet Union, 21
Sprigle, Ray, 15, 16
strikes, 25
suburbs
    de facto segregation, 52-55, 64, 83
    federal legislation, 89-90
    white flight, 58
Supreme Court
    Green v. New Kent County School Board, 48
    Keyes v. School District Number 1, 58
    McLaurin v. Oklahoma State Regents, 20
    Meredith and, 70
    Milliken v. Bradley, 64
    Plessy v. Ferguson, 11-13, 14-15, 19
    Regents of the University of California v. Bakke, The, 77-79
    Swann v. Charlotte-Mecklenburg, 55-57
    Sweatt v. Painter, 18-19
    United States v. Fordice, 76
    see also Brown v. Board of Education of Topeka, Kansas
Swann, James W., 55
Swann v. Charlotte-Mecklenburg, 55-57
Sweatt v. Painter, 18-19

teachers of African Americans, 15, 16
television, 45-46, 47, 69, 72

Tennessee, 17
Terrell, Mary Church, 34
Texas, 46, 85
Texas, University of, 18-19
Thernstrom, Abigail
    on de facto segregation, 54-55, 58
    on economic reprisals against African Americans, 40
    on extent of segregated schools, 22
    on Hurston's opposition to Brown, 91
    on importance of Brown decision, 34
    on suspension of Lucy, 58
    on white flight, 58
Thernstrom, Stephen
    on de facto segregation, 54-55, 58
    on economic reprisals against African Americans, 40
    on extent of segregated schools, 22
    on Hurston's opposition to Brown, 91
    on importance of Brown decision, 34
    on suspension of Lucy, 58
    on white flight, 58
Topeka, Kansas, 27-30, 32-34
tracking in education, 85-86

United States v. Fordice, 76
universities. See colleges and universities

Vance, Coy, 43
Vinson, Fred, 20, 30
violence
    Brown and, 35, 40-49, 50
    Clarendon County plaintiffs, 24
    desegregation in North and, 61, 62
    enforcement of slave codes, 7
    at graduate schools, 67, 72
    during Jim Crow era, 12
    during pre-Civil war era, 8-9
    voting rights and, 71
Virginia, 25-26, 39, 48, 49
"Visit to a Jim Crow School, A" (Sprigle), 16
voting rights, 71

Wallace, George Corley, 74-76
Warren, Earl, 30, 32-34, 35
Warriors Don't Cry (Pattillo), 46-47
Weisbrot, Robert, 29, 34, 57
Western states, 52-54, 58
    see also specific states
Wexler, Sanford, 24, 47
White, Byron, 76
White, Joseph L., 6, 76, 84, 91
white citizens' councils, 40, 43
white flight, 58, 64
white supremacy, 13-14, 15
Wilson, Alex, 44
Wisconsin, 54

Young Ladies and Little Misses of Color School, 8-9

Picture Credits

About the Author

Anne Wallace Sharp is the author of the adult book Gifts, a compilation of stories about hospice patients, several children's books, including Daring Pirate Women, and ten other Lucent books. In addition, she has written numerous magazine articles for both the adult and juvenile market. A retired registered nurse, Sharp has a degree in history. Her other interests include reading, traveling, and spending time with her two grandchildren, Jacob and Nicole. Sharp lives in Beavercreek, Ohio.